LOVE LYRICS FROM THE BIBLE:
A TRANSLATION AND LITERARY STUDY
OF THE SONG OF SONGS

MARCIA FALK

BIBLE AND LITERATURE
SERIES

Editor
David M. Gunn

LOVE LYRICS FROM THE BIBLE

A Translation and Literary Study of The Song of Songs

MARCIA FALK

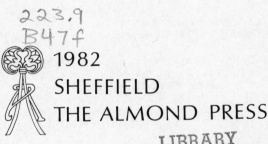

1982
SHEFFIELD
THE ALMOND PRESS

BIBLE AND LITERATURE SERIES, 4

Excerpts from the translation appeared first in the following journals: *Response, Barrow, Moment,* and *Sequoia.* The translation in its entirety but without the Hebrew text or critical study was published by Harcourt Brace Jovanovich in 1977 under the title *The Song of Songs: Love Poems from the Bible.*

British Library Cataloguing in Publication Data:
[Bible. O.T. Song of Solomon. *English. Falk. 1982*].
　　Love lyrics from the Bible: a translation and literary
　　study of the Song of Songs. — (Bible and Literature
　　series, ISSN 0260-4493;4)
　　1. Bible. O.T. Song of Solomon. *English. Falk. 1982*
　　I. Love lyrics from the Bible　　II. Falk, Marcia
　　III. Series
　　223'.9'052　　BS1487

　　ISBN 0-907459-06-4
　　ISBN 0-907459-07-2 Pbk

Published by
The Almond Press
P.O. Box 208
Sheffield S10 5DW
England

Text set in 10 point Plantin
on a Quadritek 1200 Phototypesetter

Printed in Great Britain
by Redwood Burn Limited
Trowbridge, Wiltshire
1982

IN MEMORY OF MY FATHER

אברהם אבא בן שלום דוד והינדה ז״ל

באהבה

CONTENTS

ACKNOWLEDGMENTS

THE SUBSTANCE of this work, presented here in a revised form, was originally a doctoral dissertation entitled *The Song of Songs: A Verse Translation with Exposition,* submitted to Stanford University in 1976. I am deeply grateful to my advisor, Edwin Good of the Stanford Religious Studies Department, who was the first Bible scholar with whom I studied the Song of Songs and the one who introduced me to the exciting possibilities of combining Bible scholarship with literary criticism. I am also much indebted to John Felstiner and Ronald Rebholz, my advisors in the Stanford English Department, who read the translation at various stages and guided the critical work, often making invaluable stylistic and structural suggestions. Mary K. Wakeman, of the Religion Department at the University of North Carolina at Greensboro, was also teaching at Stanford when I was beginning my study of the Song, and I thank her for her friendship then and now.

Several poets helped during the early stages of the translation. In particular, I thank Margaret Fountain Edwards, now at the University of Vermont, who generously offered me her critical eye and fine poetic sensibilities, and Kenneth Fields, of the Stanford Creative Writing Program, whose criticisms and suggestions improved both my own poetry and my translations.

From across two continents and seas, a number of Israeli scholars offered expert knowledge and kind support. I thank Nogah Hareuveni, botanist and director of Neot Kedumim: The Gardens of Israel, and Helen Frenkley, his assistant, for their help in identifying flora and fauna in the Hebrew text. I am especially grateful to Chaim Rabin, of the Hebrew Language Department at the Hebrew University, for answering my queries about obscure words in the original text; and to Moshe Greenberg, of the Bible Department at the Hebrew University, for debating with me my interpretations of the Hebrew text and for

1

encouraging me to persevere at my renditions.

I wish to acknowledge the English Department at Stanford, which provided fellowship assistance for several years; the Fulbright-Hays Foundation and the Israeli Government, which supported my research with a grant in 1973-74; the Hebrew University of Jerusalem, which gave me a postdoctoral fellowship to continue my research in 1978-79; and the Virginia Center for the Creative Arts, which offered me time and space to revise the work in 1981.

Special appreciation goes to my editor, David Gunn at the Almond Press, for his fine editorial suggestions; and to my dear friends Lillian Steinfeld and Neal Stulberg for their help in polishing this study.

For faith that I counted on at every stage, thank you, Sam. To my parents, who were my first teachers, goes my immeasurable gratitude for pointing the way.

PREFACE

ONE OF THE MOST celebrated collections of ancient love poetry, the Song of Songs (also known in English as the Song of Solomon) is the only book of love poetry in the Bible, and as such it has been the subject of much speculation and controversy. For centuries, both Jewish and Christian traditions viewed the Song as spiritual allegory, thus justifying its place in the Biblical canon; but this mode of interpretation, moving and imaginative as it may be, does not explain the text's primary level of meaning. Another centuries-old interpretation presents the Song as a drama with fixed characters, such as King Solomon and a country bride or King Solomon and two country lovers. But it is difficult to find evidence of dramatic structure in the Song: acts, scenarios, and characters are not indicated, and there is hardly a trace of coherent plot. Rather, the Song has a variety of contexts which shift frequently in no apparent dramatic sequence and within which many different kinds of voices speak. There is no reason to assume only a few fixed speakers in the Song and even less justification for viewing Solomon as a central character. Although Solomon's name is mentioned in the Hebrew title, this title was bestowed not by the Song's original author or authors but by later compilers, who were likely also responsible for giving the text its semblance of structural unity. In its earliest stages, the Song was probably not a unified work at all, but several lyric poems, each having its own integrity.

About the Song's authorship and origins very little is known. Tradition ascribes the work to King Solomon, but this view is discounted by modern scholars, who generally agree that the Song's authorship cannot be specified. In the past two centuries, scholars have hypothesized about the original context and function of the Song, proposing, for example, that it was a cycle of wedding songs or the liturgy of an ancient fertility cult. These theories, however, are not only unprovable but unconvincing, because they attempt to force the varied material in the text into single, confining molds. It is finally simpler and more illuminating to view the Song as a variegated collection of different types of lyric love poems which did not all necessarily derive from a single author or serve the same function in their original society. The stylistic similarities and repetitions among the poems are best explained as literary conventions of ancient Hebrew verse, particularly if one accepts the view that the Song was, in its earliest stages, popular oral literature. I believe it likely that the Song was orally composed and transmitted over an extended period of time before being transcribed, compiled, and finally canonized.

The reconstruction of the Hebrew text presented in this volume is based on this view of the Song; the particular division into thirty-one poems is my own, the result of literary and structural analysis. Although many scholars today view the Song as a collection, the particular decisions concerning where one poem ends and the next begins are not obvious, and no two analyses are exactly alike. The text, as we have it in the oldest complete manuscript of the Hebrew Bible, is divided into sections which may have been considered poetic units, but these divisions can hardly be regarded as definitive delineations of the *original*, orally transmitted poems. Every reconstruction is therefore a *postulation* of the original boundaries of the original poems. I divided the Hebrew text into poems as I perceived them, basing my decisions on such considerations as changes in speakers, audiences, settings, tones of voice, moods, and arguments. I then translated the Hebrew poems individually, giving each its own form in English. Thus the English poems are divided into stanzas and lines according to the demands of English poetic craft, and these prosodic divisions do not necessarily correspond to those in the Hebrew. Using the Masoretic text in *Biblia Hebraica*, with no emendations or alteration of sequence, I translated the entire text of the Song with the exception of chapter 6, verse 12, a line which has plagued commentators for centuries and for which I could arrive at no satisfactory interpretation. At the back of the book is a key indicating the Biblical chapters and verses to which each poem corresponds.

The typefaces used in the printing of the English poems require some explanation. Three different kinds of voices speak in the Song: singular male, singular female, and a group of speakers. In the original, these are usually distinguishable because in Hebrew, various parts of speech, including the pronoun 'you,' have gender and number. So, for example, if a speaker says 'I love you' in Hebrew, we know whether a man or a woman is being addressed; by assuming a heterosexual relationship (a valid assumption for the Song), we can also deduce the gender of the speaker. Without such grammatical clues, it would be difficult to know who speaks the various passages in the Song, particularly because the voices do not conform to masculine and feminine stereotypes. Because English does not convey gender grammatically as Hebrew does, the English poems are printed in three typefaces. Throughout the translation, passages spoken by a female voice are in *italic* (as in poem 1), passages spoken by a male voice are in roman (as in poem 4), and passages spoken by a group of voices or by unidentifiable speakers are in sans serif (as in poem 11).

Because many of the poems are dialogues and a few are spoken by three different voices, different typefaces appear within individual poems. Within any given poem, each typeface represents a consistent speaker; however, the typefaces do not necessarily imply consistent speakers from poem to poem. For example, the female speaker of the first stanza of poem 7 is the same as the speaker of that poem's third stanza, but not necessarily the same as the female speaker of poem 8.

                                   *   *   *

But why this new translation of the Song, a book that has been translated, interpreted, arranged, and — to use Franz Rosenzweig's image — 'convulsed' many times? By far the most acclaimed English version is that found in the King James Bible, which, although it treats the Song no differently from Biblical prose, achieves a level of grace and eloquence that earns it a unique place among English classics. Still, from the perspective of scholarship, the King James Version is long outdated. Our understanding of the Hebrew text has changed considerably since the time of the King James, and one of the offshoots of modern research has been a series of new Bible translations. Some of the new English Bibles which have appeared in the last few decades are: the Revised Standard Version (1946-52), The Jerusalem Bible (1966), The New American Bible (1970), The New English Bible (1970), and The Five Megilloth and Jonah by the Jewish Publication Society (1969). While all these versions make gestures to indicate that the original is verse, primarily by breaking the text into sections and lines, they lack real poetic texture and density, necessary for faithful rendition of the Hebrew. Hence the need to go one step further, to combine scholarship with conscious poetic craft and sensibility. This translation is an attempt to fill that need.

I was aware, from the outset, of the great impact that the King James Version has had on the ears of English readers. Rather than try to echo its rhythms or diction, I set out to create an entirely fresh version that would open the locked gardens of the Hebrew. My aim was to probe the roots of the original and uncover resonances lost in other translations, but *not* to 'Hebraize' English or mimic the aesthetic techniques of Hebrew verse. Rather than writing 'translationese,' I tried to write the best poetry I could.

All translations are, by necessity, interpretations. My interpretations are based on linguistic investigations and literary analysis, which are discussed in the critical study that comprises the second half of this book. Chapter one of this study presents a way of thinking about literary translation and explains my approach to translating the Song; chapter two presents the advantages of viewing the Song as a collection rather than as a structural unity, and explains the principles behind my reconstruction of the text. Chapters three, four, and five probe other literary questions relevant to the structure and content of the Song, and chapter six treats selected matters of interpretation in the individual poems. The entire volume is a translator's study, that is, an exploration of aspects of the text that revealed themselves in the process of translation. For that reason, reference is made as needed to both the Hebrew text and the English translations. For readers who know no Hebrew, word-for-word translations are provided whenever the Hebrew is cited and its meaning is not apparent from the context. All Hebrew words in the study are also presented in transliterated form, so that the non-Hebrew reader may sense their shape and sound. Because of the specific focus of this work, many issues normally treated by Bible scholars, such as the origin and authorship of the text, its time of composition, original life setting, and liturgical functions, are barely touched upon here. Discussions of such issues may be found in the Bible introductions and commentaries listed in the bibliography.

As I explain in the first chapter of the study, there can be no truly literal translation of a literary work. Although none of my translations even strives to be literal, all are attempts to draw close to the meanings, intentions, and spirit of the original. My aim has been fidelity — not to isolated images, but to the meanings of images in their original cultural contexts and to the effects they might have had on their earliest audience. Thus, at times, my renditions will seem to depart radically from other, more literal versions.

For example, in chapter 1, verse 9 of the Hebrew (the opening lines of my poem 4), a woman is compared to a mare in Pharaoh's chariotry. A puzzling image: only stallions, never mares, drew chariots. But the Egyptians' enemies set mares loose in war to drive the Pharaoh's stallions wild, and this is the crux of the metaphor. The woman is not simply a beautiful creature; she is as alluring as 'a mare among stallions.' Thus the image unfolds on two levels and paradox is implied: the woman is a graceful, quiet profile, yet also a dangerous, captivating power. Seen this way, the image also ties with the rest of the poem, which is built on the subtle paradox of the love relationship: although the beloved is beautiful just as she is, the speaker, wanting to share love, offers to adorn her with his own gifts.

The poems in this book are a gift back to their source and an attempt to share in the tradition.

THE SONG OF SONGS
AS THIRTY-ONE POEMS
AND THE
ENGLISH TRANSLATIONS

שיר השירים אשר לשלמה

THE SONG OF SONGS

1

ישקני מנשיקות פיהו
כי טובים דדיך מיין
לריח שמניך טובים
שמן תורק שמך
על כן עלמות אהבוך

משכני אחריך נרוצה
הביאני המלך חדריו
נגילה ונשמחה בך
נזכירה דדיך מיין
מישרים אהבוך

2

שחורה אני ונאוה
בנות ירושלם
כאהלי קדר
כיריעות שלמה

אל תראוני שאני שחרחרת
ששזפתני השמש

בני אמי נחרו בי
שמני נטרה את הכרמים
כרמי שלי לא נטרתי

Poem 1

O for your kiss! For your love
More enticing than wine,
For your scent and sweet name—
For all this they love you.

Take me away to your room,
Like a king to his rooms—
We'll rejoice there with wine.
No wonder they love you!

Poem 2

Yes, I am black! and radiant—
O city women watching me—
As black as Kedar's goathair tents
Or Solomon's fine tapestries.

Will you disrobe me with your stares?
The eyes of many morning suns
Have pierced my skin, and now I shine
Black as the light before the dawn.

And I have faced the angry glare
Of others, even my mother's sons
Who sent me out to watch their vines
While I neglected all my own.

3

הגידה לי שאהבה נפשי
איכה תרעה
איכה תרביץ בצהרים
שלמה אהיה כעטיה
על עדרי חבריך

אם לא תדעי לך
היפה בנשים
צאי לך בעקבי הצאן
ורעי את גדיתיך
על משכנות הרעים

4

לססתי ברכבי פרעה
דמיתיך רעיתי
נאוו לחייך בתרים
צוארך בחרוזים
תורי זהב נעשה לך
עם נקדות הכסף

Poem 3

Tell me, my love, where you feed your sheep
And where you rest in the afternoon,
For why should I go searching blindly
Among the flocks of your friends?

If you don't know, O lovely woman,
Follow the tracks that the sheep have made
And feed your own little goats and lambs
In the fields where the shepherds lie.

Poem 4

Like a mare among stallions,
You lure, I am held

      your cheeks framed with braids
      your neck traced with shells

I'll adorn you with gold
And with silver bells

5

עד שהמלך במסבו
נרדי נתן ריחו
צרור המר דודי לי
בין שדי ילין
אשכל הכפר דודי לי
בכרמי עין גדי

6

הנך יפה רעיתי
הנך יפה
עיניך יונים

הנך יפה דודי
אף נעים
אף ערשנו רעננה
קרות בתינו ארזים
רחיטנו ברותים

Poem 5

Until the king returns
    I lie in fragrance,
Sweet anticipation
    Of his entrance.

Between my breasts he'll lie—
    Sachet of spices,
Spray of blossoms plucked
    From the oasis.

Poem 6

How fine
you are, my love,
your eyes
like doves'.

How fine
are you, my lover,
what joy
we have together.

How green
our bed of leaves,
our rafters of cedars,
our juniper eaves.

7

אני חבצלת השרון
שושנת העמקים

כשושנה בין החוחים
כן רעיתי בין הבנות

כתפוח בעצי היער
כן דודי בין הבנים
בצלו חמדתי וישבתי
ופריו מתוק לחכי

8

הביאני אל בית היין
ודגלו עלי אהבה
סמכוני באשישות
רפדוני בתפוחים
כי חולת אהבה אני

שמאלו תחת לראשי
וימינו תחבקני

השבעתי אתכם בנות ירושלם
בצבאות או באילות השדה
אם תעירו ואם תעוררו
את האהבה עד שתחפץ

Poem 7

In sandy earth or deep
In valley soil
I grow, a wildflower thriving
On your love.

Narcissus in the brambles,
Brightest flower—
I choose you from all others
For my love.

Sweet fruit tree growing wild
Within the thickets—
I blossom in your shade
And taste your love.

Poem 8

He brings me to the winehall,
Gazing at me with love.

Feed me raisincakes and quinces!
For I am sick with love.

O for his arms around me,
Beneath me and above.

O women of the city,
Swear by the wild field doe

Not to wake or rouse us
Till we fulfill our love.

9

קול דודי
הנה זה בא
מדלג על ההרים
מקפץ על הגבעות
דומה דודי לצבי
או לעפר האילים
הנה זה עומר
אחר כתלנו
משגיח מן החלנות
מציץ מן החרכים

ענה דודי ואמר לי

קומי לך רעיתי
יפתי ולכי לך
כי הנה הסתו עבר
הגשם חלף הלך לו
הנצנים נראו בארץ
עת הזמיר הגיע
וקול התור נשמע בארצנו
התאנה חנטה פגיה
והגפנים סמדר נתנו ריח
קומי לכי רעיתי
יפתי ולכי לך

Poem 9

The sound of my lover
coming from the hills
quickly, like a deer
upon the mountains

Now at my windows,
walking by the walls,
here at the lattices
he calls—

Come with me,
my love,
come away

For the long wet months are past,
the rains have fed the earth
and left it bright with blossoms

Birds wing in the low sky,
dove and songbird singing
in the open air above

Earth nourishing tree and vine,
green fig and tender grape,
green and tender fragrance

Come with me,
my love,
come away

10

יונתי בחגוי הסלע
בסתר המדרגה
הראיני את מראיך
השמיעיני את קולך
כי קולך ערב
ומראיך נאוה

11

אחזו לנו שועלים
שועלים קטנים
מחבלים כרמים
וכרמינו סמדר

Poem 10

My dove
    in the clefts
        of the rocks
    the secret
        of steep ravines

Come let me look at you
Come let me hear you

    Your voice clear as water
    Your beautiful body

Poem 11

Catch the foxes!
    the little foxes
    among the vines
Catch the foxes!
    the quick little foxes
    raiding the new grapes
    on our vines

12

דודי לי ואני לו
הרעה בשושנים

עד שיפוח היום
ונסו הצללים
סב דמה לך
דודי לצבי
או לעפר האילים
על הרי בתר

13

על משכבי בלילות
בקשתי את שאהבה נפשי
בקשתיו ולא מצאתיו

אקומה נא ואסובבה בעיר
בשוקים וברחבות
אבקשה את שאהבה נפשי
בקשתיו ולא מצאתיו

מצאוני השמרים הסבבים בעיר
את שאהבה נפשי ראיתם
כמעט שעברתי מהם
עד שמצאתי את שאהבה נפשי

אחזתיו ולא ארפנו
עד שהביאתיו אל בית אמי
ואל חדר הורתי

השבעתי אתכם בנות ירושלם
בצבאות או באילות השדה
אם תעירו ואם תעוררו
את האהבה עד שתחפץ

Poem 12

My lover turns to me,
I turn to him,
Who leads his flock to feed
Among the flowers.

Until the day is over
And the shadows flee,
Turn round, my lover,
Go quickly, and be
Like deer or gazelles
In the clefts of the hills.

Poem 13

At night in bed, I want him—
The one I love is not here.

I'll rise and search the city,
Through the streets and squares

Until the city watchmen
Find me wandering there

And I ask them—have you seen him?
The one I love is not here.

When they have gone, I find him
And I won't let him go

Until he's in my mother's home,
The room where I was born.

O women of the city,
Swear by the wild field doe

Not to wake or rouse us
Till we fulfill our love.

שיר השירים

14

מי זאת עלה מן המדבר
כתימרות עשן
מקטרת מור ולבונה
מכל אבקת רוכל

הנה מטתו שלשלמה
ששים גברים סביב לה
מגברי ישראל
כלם אחזי חרב
מלמדי מלחמה
איש חרבו על ירכו
מפחד בלילות

אפריון עשה לו
המלך שלמה
מעצי הלבנון
עמודיו עשה כסף
רפידתו זהב
מרכבו ארגמן
תוכו רצוף אהבה
מבנות ירושלם

צאינה וראינה בנות ציון
במלך שלמה
בעטרה שעטרה לו אמו
ביום חתנתו
וביום שמחת לבו

Poem 14

Who is this approaching, up from the desert
In columns of smoke, fragrant with incense,
Rare spices and herbs of the wandering merchants?

Behold, it appears—the king's own procession
Attended by sixty of Israel's warriors,
Swords at their thighs to meet the night's dangers.

A carriage of cedar with pillars of silver,
Gold floor, purple cushions, all made to his orders
And fashioned with love by Jerusalem's daughters.

Go out and see, O Jerusalem's daughters!
Crowned by his mother, the king in his carriage
This day of rejoicing, this day of his marriage.

15

הנך יפה רעיתי
הנך יפה
עיניך יונים
מבעד לצמתך

שערך כעדר העזים
שגלשו מהר גלעד

שניך כעדר הקצובות
שעלו מן הרחצה
שכלם מתאימות
ושכלה אין בהם

כחוט השני שפתתיך
ומדבריך נאוה

כפלח הרמון רקתך
מבעד לצמתך

כמגדל דויד צוארך
בנוי לתלפיות
אלף המגן תלוי עליו
כל שלטי הגבורים

שני שדיך כשני עפרים
תאומי צביה
הרועים בשושנים

עד שיפוח היום
ונסו הצללים
אלך לי אל הר המור
ואל גבעת הלבונה

כלך יפה רעיתי
ומום אין בך

Poem 15

How fine
you are, my love,
your eyes like doves'
behind your veil

Your hair—
as black as goats
winding down the slopes

Your teeth—
a flock of sheep
rising from the stream
in twos, each with its twin

Your lips—
like woven threads
of crimson silk

A gleam of pomegranate—
your forehead
through your veil

Your neck—
a tower
adorned with shields

Your breasts—
twin fawns
in fields of flowers

Until
the day is over,
shadows gone,

I'll go
up to the hills
of fragrant bloom

How fine
you are, my love,
my perfect one

16

אתי מלבנון כלה
אתי מלבנון תבואי
תשורי מראש אמנה
מראש שניר וחרמון
ממענות אריות
מהררי נמרים

17

לבבתני אחתי כלה
לבבתני באחד מעיניך
באחד ענק מצורניך

מה יפו דדיך אחתי כלה
מה טבו דדיך מיין
וריח שמניך מכל בשמים

נפת תטפנה שפתותיך כלה
דבש וחלב תחת לשונך
וריח שלמתיך כריח לבנון

Poem 16

With me, my bride of the mountains,
Come away with me, come away!

Come down from the peaks of the mountains,
From the perilous Lebanon caves,

From the lairs where lions crouch hidden,
Where leopards watch nightly for prey,

Look down, look down and come away!

Poem 17

With one flash of your eyes, you excite me,
One jewel on your neck stirs my heart,
    O my sister, my bride.

Your love, more than wine, is enticing,
Your fragrance is finer than spices,
    My sister, my bride.

Your lips, sweet with nectar, invite me
To honey and milk on your tongue,
    O my sister, my bride.

And even your clothing is fragrant
As wind from the Lebanon mountains,
    My sister, my bride.

18

גן נעול אחתי כלה
גל נעול מעין חתום
שלחיך פרדס רמונים
עם פרי מגדים
כפרים עם נרדים
נרד וכרכם קנה וקנמון
עם כל עצי לבונה
מר ואהלות
עם כל ראשי בשמים
מעין גנים
באר מים חיים
ונזלים מן לבנון

עורי צפון ובואי תימן
הפיחי גני יזלו בשמיו
יבא דודי לגנו
ויאכל פרי מגדיו

באתי לגני אחתי כלה
אריתי מורי עם בשמי
אכלתי יערי עם דבשי
שתיתי ייני עם חלבי

אכלו רעים
שתו ושכרו דודים

Poem 18

Enclosed and hidden, you are a garden,
A still pool, a fountain.

Stretching your limbs, you open—
A field of pomegranates blooms,

Treasured fruit among the blossoms,
Henna, sweet cane, bark, and saffron,

Fragrant woods and succulents,
The finest spices and perfumes.

Living water, you are a fountain,
A well, a river flowing from the mountains.

Come, north winds and south winds!
Breathe upon my garden,

Bear its fragrance to my lover,
Let him come and share its treasures.

My bride, my sister, I have come
To gather spices in my garden,

To taste wild honey with my wine,
Milk and honey with my wine.

Feast, drink—and drink deeply—lovers!

19

אני ישנה ולבי ער
קול דודי דופק

פתחי לי אחתי רעיתי
יונתי תמתי
שראשי נמלא טל
קוצותי רסיסי לילה

פשטתי את כתנתי
איככה אלבשנה
רחצתי את רגלי
איככה אטנפם

דודי שלח ידו מן החר
ומעי המו עליו
קמתי אני לפתח לדודי
וידי נטפו מור
ואצבעתי מור עבר
על כפות המנעול
פתחתי אני לדודי
ודודי חמק עבר
נפשי יצאה בדברו
בקשתיהו ולא מצאתיהו
קראתיו ולא ענני
מצאני השמרים הסבבים בעיר
הכוני פצעוני
נשאו את רדידי מעלי
שמרי החמות

השבעתי אתכם בנות ירושלם
אם תמצאו את דודי
מה תגידו לו
שחולת אהבה אני

מה דודך מדוד
היפה בנשים
מה דודך מדוד
שככה השבעתנו

דודי צח ואדום
דגול מרבבה

Poem 19

I sleep, but my heart stirs,
restless,
          and dreams . . .

My lover's voice here, at the door—

Open, my love, my sister,
my dove, my perfect one,
for my hair is soaked with the night.

Should I get up, get dressed, and dirty my feet?

My love thrusts his hand at the latch
and my heart leaps for him.
I rise to open for my love,
my hands dripping perfume on the lock.
I open, but he has gone.

I run out after him, calling, but he is gone.

The men who roam the streets,
guarding the walls,
beat me and tear away my robe.

O women of the city,
Swear to me!
If you find my lover
You will say
That I am sick with love.

Who is your love
And why do you bind us by oath?

My love is radiant
As gold or crimson,
Hair in waves of black
Like wings of ravens.

ראשו כתם פז
קווצותיו תלתלים
שחרות כעורב

עיניו כיונים
על אפיקי מים
רחצות בחלב
ישבות על מלאת

לחיו כערוגת הבשם
מגדלות מרקחים

שפתותיו שושנים
נטפות מור עבר

ידיו גלילי זהב
ממלאים בתרשיש

מעיו עשת שן
מעלפת ספירים

שוקיו עמודי שש
מיסדים על אדני פז

מראהו כלבנון
בחור כארזים

חכו ממתקים
וכלו מחמדים

זה דודי וזה רעי
בנות ירושלם

אנה הלך דודך
היפה בנשים
אנה פנה דודך
ונבקשנו עמך

דודי ירד לגנו
לערוגות הבשם
לרעות בגנים
וללקט שושנים

אני לדודי ודודי לי
הרעה בשושנים

Eyes like doves, afloat
Upon the water,
Bathed in milk, at rest
On brimming pools.

Cheeks like beds of spices,
Banks of flowers,
Lips like lilies, sweet
And wet with dew.

Studded with jewels, his arms
Are round and golden,
His belly smooth as ivory,
Bright with gems.

Set in gold, his legs,
Two marble columns—
He stands as proud as cedars
In the mountains.

Man of pleasure—sweet
To taste his love!
Friend and lover chosen
For my love.

Beautiful woman,
Where has your lover gone to?
Where has he gone?
We'll help you look for him.

My love has gone to walk
Within his garden—
To feed his sheep and there
To gather flowers.

I turn to meet my love,
He'll turn to me,
Who leads his flock to feed
Among the flowers.

ERRATUM

The first five quatrains on page 37 should appear in italic typeface.

20

יפה את רעיתי כתרצה
נאוה כירושלם
אימה כנדגלות
הסבי עיניך מנגדי
שהם הרהיבני

שערך כעדר העזים
שגלשו מן הגלעד
שניך כעדר הרחלים
שעלו מן הרחצה
שכלם מתאימות
ושכלה אין בהם
כפלח הרמון רקתך
מבעד לצמתך

ששים המה מלכות
ושמנים פילגשים
ועלמות אין מספר
אחת היא יונתי תמתי
אחת היא לאמה
ברה היא ליולדתה
ראוה בנות ויאשרוה
מלכות ופילגשים ויהללוה

מי זאת הנשקפה כמו שחר
יפה כלבנה
ברה כחמה
אימה כנדגלות

Poem 20

Striking as Tirza
    you are, my love,
Bright as Jerusalem,
    frightening as visions!
Lower your eyes
    for they make me tremble

Your hair—as black as goats
    winding down the slopes
Your teeth—a flock of sheep
    rising from the stream
    in twos, each with its twin
A gleam of pomegranate—
    your forehead through your veil

Sixty queens, eighty brides,
    endless numbers of women—
One is my dove, my perfect one,
    pure as an only child—
Women see her
    and sing of her joy,
Queens and brides
    chant her praise

Who is she? staring
    down like the dawn's eye,
Bright as the white moon,
    pure as the hot sun,
Frightening as visions!

21

אל גנת אגוז ירדתי
לראות באבי הנחל
לראות הפרחה הגפן
הנצו הרמנים

לא ידעתי נפשי שמתני מרכבות עמי נדיב

22

שובי שובי השולמית
שובי שובי ונחזה בך

מה תחזו בשולמית
כמחלת המחנים

מה יפו פעמיך בנעלים
בת נדיב

חמוקי ירכיך כמו חלאים
מעשה ידי אמן

שררך אגן הסהר
אל יחסר המזג

בטנך ערמת חטים
סוגה בשושנים

שני שדיך כשני עפרים
תאמי צביה

צוארך כמגדל השן

עיניך ברכות בחשבון
על שער בת רבים

אפך כמגדל הלבנון
צופה פני דמשק

ראשך עליך ככרמל
ודלת ראשך כארגמן
מלך אסור ברהטים

Poem 21

Walking through the walnut orchard,
Looking for the signs of spring:
The pomegranates—have they flowered?
The grapevines—are they blossoming?

Poem 22

Dance for us, princess, dance,
    as we watch and chant!

*What will you see as I move
    in the dance of love?*

Your graceful, sandalled feet,
Your thighs—two spinning jewels,
Your hips—a bowl of nectar
    brimming full

Your belly—golden wheat
Adorned with daffodils,
Your breasts—two fawns, the twins
    of a gazelle

Your neck—an ivory tower,
Your eyes—two silent pools,
Your face—a tower that overlooks
    the hills

Your head—majestic mountain
Crowned with purple hair,
Captivating kings
    within its locks

23

מה יפית ומה נעמת
אהבה בתענוגים

זאת קומתך דמתה לתמר
ושדיך לאשכלות

אמרתי אעלה בתמר
אחזה בסנסניו

ויהיו נא שדיך כאשכלות הגפן
וריח אפך כתפוחים

וחכך כיין הטוב
הולך לדודי למישרים
דובב שפתי ישנים

24

אני לדודי ועלי תשוקתו

לכה דודי נצא השדה
נלינה בכפרים
נשכימה לכרמים
נראה אם פרחה הגפן
פתח הסמדר
הנצו הרמונים

שם אתן את דדי לך
הדודאים נתנו ריח
ועל פתחינו כל מגדים
חדשים גם ישנים
דודי צפנתי לך

Poem 23

Of all pleasure, how sweet
Is the taste of love!

There you stand like a palm,
Your breasts clusters of dates.

Shall I climb that palm
And take hold of the boughs?

Your breasts will be tender
As clusters of grapes,

Your breath will be sweet
As the fragrance of quince,

And your mouth will awaken
All sleeping desire

Like wine that entices
The lips of new lovers.

Poem 24

Turning to him, who meets me with desire—

Come, love, let us go out to the open fields
And spend our night lying where the henna blooms,
Rising early to leave for the near vineyards
Where the vines flower, opening tender buds,
And the pomegranate boughs unfold their blossoms.

There among blossom and vine I will give you my love,
Musk of the violet mandrakes spilled upon us . . .
And returning, finding our doorways piled with fruits,
The best of the new-picked and the long-stored,
My love, I will give you all I have saved for you.

25

מי יתנך כאח לי
יונק שדי אמי
אמצאך בחוץ אשקך
גם לא יבוזו לי
אנהגך אביאך
אל בית אמי
תלמדני
אשקך מיין הרקח
מעסיס רמני

שמאלו תחת ראשי
וימינו תחבקני

השבעתי אתכם בנות ירושלם
מה תעירו ומה תעררו
את האהבה עד שתחפץ

26

מי זאת עלה מן המדבר
מתרפקת על דודה

Poem 25

Oh, if you were my brother
Nursed at my mother's breast,

I'd kiss you in the streets
And never suffer scorn.

I'd bring you to my mother's home
(My mother teaches me)

And give you wine and nectar
From my pomegranates.

O for his arms around me,
Beneath me and above!

O women of the city,
Swear by the wild field doe

Not to wake or rouse us
Till we fulfill our love.

Poem 26

Who is this approaching,
    up from the wilderness,
        arm on her lover's arm?

27

תחת התפוח עוררתיך
שמה חבלתך אמך
שמה חבלה ילדתך

28

שימני כחותם על לבך
כחותם על זרועך

כי עזה כמות אהבה
קשה כשאול קנאה
רשפיה רשפי אש
שלהבתיה

מים רבים לא יוכלו
לכבות את האהבה
ונהרות לא ישטפוה

אם יתן איש
את כל הון ביתו באהבה
בוז יבוזו לו

Poem 27

Under the quince tree
      you woke
      to my touch
there
      where she conceived
      where she who carried
      and bore you
conceived

Poem 28

Stamp me in your heart,
Upon your limbs,
Sear my emblem deep
Into your skin.

For love is strong as death,
Harsh as the grave.
Its tongues are flames, a fierce
And holy blaze.

Endless seas and floods,
Torrents and rivers
Never put out love's
Infinite fires.

Those who think that wealth
Can buy them love
Only play the fool
And meet with scorn.

29

אחות לנו קטנה
ושדים אין לה
מה נעשה לאחתנו
ביום שידבר בה

אם חומה היא
נבנה עליה טירת כסף
ואם דלת היא
נצור עליה לוח ארז

אני חומה
ושדי כמגדלות
אז הייתי בעיניו
כמוצאת שלום

30

כרם היה לשלמה
בבעל המון
נתן את הכרם לנטרים
איש יבא בפריו
אלף כסף

כרמי שלי לפני
האלף לך שלמה
ומאתים לנטרים את פריו

Poem 29

We have a young sister
Whose breasts are but flowers.
What shall we do
When the time comes for suitors?

If she's a wall
We'll build turrets of silver,
But if she's a door
We will plank her with cedar.

I am a wall
And my breasts are towers!
So I have found peace
Here with my lover.

Poem 30

The king has a vineyard
Whose fruit is worth silver.
I have a vineyard—
Its fruit is my own.

Have your wealth, Solomon!
Keep all your vineyards,
Whose yield you must share
With your watchmen and guards.

31

היושבת בגנים
חברים מקשיבים לקולך
השמיעיני

ברח דודי
ודמה לך לצבי
או לעפר האילים
על הרי בשמים

Poem 31

Woman
of the gardens,
of the voice
friends listen for,
will you let me hear you?

Go—
go now, my love,
be quick
as a gazelle
on the fragrant hills!

A Literary Study
of the
Song of Songs

ONE

TRANSLATION AS A JOURNEY

All journeys have secret destinations of which the traveler is unaware.[1]

ALL TRANSLATIONS necessarily imply departures from what might be posited as literal readings. I say 'what might be posited' because the literal level is a hypothetical concept; although we speak of some translations as more literal than others, there are no *truly* literal translations of literary texts.[2] It is often impossible to find an exact equivalent for even a single word; how can one hope to translate a string of words without altering some element of syntax, or semantics, or sound? Indeed, the translator faces choices — often very close ones — at every step along the way.

Choosing one word over others, one inevitably sacrifices overtones and connotations. Thus we often speak of 'losing in translation'; yet it is also true that there are gains. Translation is a kind of journey: a 'carrying across' from one cultural-linguistic context to another. While experienced travelers know to discard unnecessary baggage along the way, they also often find new acquisitions. So, too, when texts are carried from one language to another, the particular gains and losses are not predictable. Deciding to translate means willingly risking departure as the first step in a not entirely foreseeable sequence.

Having departed from a text by deciding to translate it, by envisioning its shape and sound in a language not its own, the

[1] Martin Buber, 'The Life of the Hasidim' in *Hasidism and Modern Man*, trans. Maurice Friedman (New York: Harper & Row, 1966), p. 102.

[2] In subsequent chapters, I use the words 'literal' and 'literally' to refer to word-for-word translations of isolated words, phrases, and lines, intended to be as exact as possible. These are offered mainly to explain points about the original to the non-Hebrew reader, and to clarify specific departures in various translations, primarily my own.

translator's next move is toward the text again, into its subtleties and details, its flaws, peculiarities, and perfections. The enveloping mists are lifted; the relationship comes down to earth; it will not do to admire at a distance any more; one must see the rocks and ravines as well as the contours of the mountains. But then, once intimacy is established, the translator leaves again, taking another step away from the text, back into the self, to begin the utterance that will be the new work. For the translation too must have a life, one that breathes to its own rhythms; it cannot exist without its own nourishing atmosphere. Thus the process of translation is a to-and-fro voyage, toward and away from the shores of the text, until finally there is new land on which to disembark.[3]

Yet we speak of fidelity in translation; we assume that this is the ultimate aim. Fidelity suggests attachment and commitment: how is such loyalty reconciled with all the leavetaking a translator must do?

There is no contradiction here. Fidelity means being close, not clinging to surfaces. It means fulfilling a trust, an obligation to be true to the relationship between self and other. A faithful translation of a text accurately represents its best and fullest appreciation by a reader. If that reader is sensitive, the appreciation will not be idiosyncratic, but it will necessarily be subjective. There is no way around it: translation emerges from interpretation, that 'going between' which can never be wholly objective but which strives for truth all the same.

Each translator thus defines the essential relationship between text and reader; this is what must be spoken anew. Some translators, for example, emphasize semantic content, while others aim to recreate tone. Usually, one strives for a balance among the many aspects that form the essence of text, but each balance is unique; there is no single formula for faithful translation.

The concept of fidelity is even more complex with poetic texts, for here the choices between form and content are more exclusive of each other. Suppose one wanted to translate a classical Chinese poem into modern English. One choice might be to render it in an analogous form, such as a sonnet, although this might mean sacrificing up some

[3] I am indebted to Leo Spitzer for his notion of the 'to-and-from voyage' in literary interpretation, which I have extended by analogy. Spitzer speaks of the 'voyage from certain outward details to the inner center and back again to other details' as the process by which we come to know a text. See 'Linguistics and Literary History' in *Linguistics and Literary History: Essays in Stylistics* (Princeton: Princeton Univ. Press, 1948), pp. 19-20.

of the original imagery. On the other hand, one could argue that a T'ang dynasty poem is by definition formal, whereas a modern English poem is not, and that therefore the effects of meter and rhyme in a modern sonnet are wholly different from those of syllable count and parallelism in classical Chinese verse. The arguments about what constitutes faithful translation of poetic texts have to do with how we understand the very nature of poetry — by no means a closed question.

Perhaps no factor is more challenging to the translator than extreme historical distance, for what we think we understand of ancient texts often proves insufficient when we try to translate. When translating ancient literature, one is often forced to rely on the text alone, much as the New Critics would have us do by choice. But when one *has* the choice, it is easier; with limited knowledge of the cultural context of a work, one may find it difficult to determine its effects or guess at its intentions. And when there is nowhere to turn for the very meanings of words which have gone out of use, the translator's task can be quite frustrating.

The translator can, however, turn this disadvantage into a positive challenge. For now the need for subjective involvement is intensified; there is no choice but to engage the self entirely to speculate about the meaning of the textual object. The results are conclusions or, more precisely, postulations, about what the text may have meant, how it may have been perceived in its own time. Above all, what must be acknowledged is that faithful translation, like original linguistic creativity, is a deeply human enterprise. The relationship between translator and text is analogous to that between writer and subject matter: the same intense bearing of the self upon perception of the other is necessary to make a work of art happen.

My translation of the Song of Songs, a poetic text at least two millennia old, and for which there are no native speakers today,[4] is the result of a quite personal engagement. The process began with listening, moved into study and research, took me to cautious speculation, and led to certain choices: subjective but not arbitrary interpretations. These interpretations were the seedlings I then took back to plant in the new terrain of my own language.

                                *   *   *

[4] Although there is a new generation of Hebrew speakers, theirs is not the language of the Bible, and they too must study Biblical Hebrew to receive its meaning.

But why did I embark on such a venture? Why a new translation of the Song? Why not stop with the King James Version, or the scores of lesser versions which have followed it?

The answer is that, although the King James is a classic, there *is* a need for a new translation: the King James is outdated in many ways, and nothing has fulfilled the need it once satisfied. Modern understanding of Biblical prosody reveals that the King James Version, despite its eloquence, does Biblical verse a disservice by treating it no differently from Biblical prose. We cannot discern, from the King James Version, the original poem units in the Song; nor do we sense from it the Hebrew poetic line. The long, cadenced lines of the King James correspond not to the actual breath/syntax units of the Hebrew, but to the demarcated 'verses' (*p^esuqim*). Probably because of this, English readers tend to think of Biblical verse as extenuated and oracular — like the style of Walt Whitman or Christopher Smart. Nothing could be less true. The Hebrew lines are relatively short units of two, three, or four beats, and anywhere from two to five such lines make up the average Biblical verse. (The next chapter, which treats the literary structure of the Song, explains further the distinction between poetic lines and *p^esuqim*, and also takes up the question of how one delineates the original poems in the Hebrew.)

My version does not attempt to mimic the rhythms of Hebrew verse, for this would be unnatural in English. English, an analytic language, requires more words to express thought than does the synthetic language of the Bible, which can, for example, incorporate preposition, article, and noun, or subject, verb, and accusative pronoun, into a single word. English cannot express whole thought units in two or three beats, and to force it to do so would violate its own natural rhythms. To imitate the long-lined style of the King James, on the other hand, would reinforce a misconception about Biblical verse. My lines of verse are therefore a deliberate departure from the styles of both the King James Version and the original Hebrew text. The lines in my version are of variable length, divided according to the demands of English verse, while still intended to reflect (not mimic) the quick, delicate qualities of the Hebrew. About the style and forms of the poems I will say more shortly.

In addition, as I noted in the preface, the King James Version is outdated from the perspective of scholarship. Its many inaccuracies are apparent to modern scholars of the Hebrew, and some of its errors are known also to English readers: a classic example is 'the voice of the turtle' (2:12) for 'the voice of the turtledove.' It is not enough, however, to correct the errors in an attempt to update the King James Version. The Revised Standard Version of the Bible is one attempt to do that; instructively, it has not had nearly the impact on English readers that the King James has had. The King James remains more known, recited, and loved in the twentieth century because it succeeds as literature in English; the Revised Standard Version, by comparison, pales as a literary text. Like most twentieth-century Bible translations, the Revised Standard Version speaks not in a contemporary English voice but in a stilted echo of archaic rhythms and diction; the language does not reveal itself as true, the voice has little integrity. Even the more recent versions, which consciously attempt to be less archaic, have not gone far enough, for they have not succeeded in creating a whole, authentic voice of their own. The translators of the King James Version, on the other hand, seem not to be imitating, but creating; they seem to strive for the best literary style of their own time. This makes their version moving and authentic; it is what gives it integrity. In this sense it is also more faithful to the original than the modern versions which attempt to update it, because it conveys far more of the immediacy and accessibility that the Hebrew text must have had in its original milieu. In other words, the King James Version, unlike many modern versions of the Bible, reads not like a translation but like literature. The need for a modern translation of the Song — one that incorporates the insights of new scholarship yet reads like authentic poetry — is what I attempted to fill.

I also stated in the preface that I did not try to 'Hebraize' English. Hebraized English is inauthentic language — neither Hebrew nor English — which makes unfaithful translation. The original verse is not strained or awkward, and it seems fair to expect the translation to be equally at home in its own language. I raise this issue not so much to make a point about other English versions (although many English Bibles seem unconsciously to Hebraize the language by imposing such things as Hebrew word order upon English), but to distinguish my concept of faithful translation from that of the German Bible translators Martin Buber and Franz Rosenzweig. The Buber-Rosenzweig translation of the Hebrew Bible, begun in 1925 and completed by Buber in 1961, is, in many ways, a unique and monumental work in the history of Bible translation.[5] Although it is not well known to English readers, it raises issues that no other translation does, and deserves for that reason at least minimal consideration here.

The primary aim of the Buber-Rosenzweig translation was to revive the spoken quality of the Hebrew text for a contemporary German audience. In order to do this, the translators took considerable license with the German language, deliberately wrenching it from its own natural rhythms in an attempt to startle, and thus awaken, the ear of the German hearer. Buber stated his intention as follows: 'German spoken forms can never reproduce the Hebrew spoken forms, but, growing out of analogous impulses and exerting analogous effects, they can correspond to them in German, render them into German.'[6] In other words, the principle behind their translation was 'not to Germanize the Hebrew but to Hebraize the German.'[7]

While Buber and Rosenzweig began with an appreciation of the text as spoken, they ended up with a German version which is, to a great extent, unspeakable. That is, it is nothing like the normal spoken German of its time. As the eminent scholar of Jewish philosophy Gershom Scholem put it in a lecture given at the completion of the translation, 'the language into which you translated was not that of everyday speech nor that of German literature in the 1920's.'[8] Unfortunately, the Buber-Rosenzweig translation never had a chance to test itself with German speakers because the audience for whom it was intended, the German Jewish population, was all but totally extinguished in the Holocaust. As Scholem continued in his moving speech:

[5] For knowledge of the aims and principles behind the Buber-Rosenzweig translation, I am indebted to the work of Everett Fox, much of which he shared with me in correspondence and conversation. Fox's doctoral dissertation, 'Technical Aspects of the Translation of Genesis of Martin Buber and Franz Rosenzweig' (Dept. of Near Eastern and Judaic Studies, Brandeis, 1974), provides otherwise unavailable exegesis and background of this text. In addition, Fox's own Biblical translation, *In the Beginning: An English Rendition of the Book of Genesis (Response,* No. 14 [Summer, 1972], entire), modeled after the work of Buber and Rosenzweig, provides exemplification of the Buber-Rosenzweig method for non-German readers. The 'Translator's Afterword' in *In the Beginning* gives a brief synopsis of the history and purpose of the Buber-Rosenzweig translation.

[6] Martin Buber, 'Ueber die Wortwahl in einer Verdeutschung der Schrift' (1930) in *Die Schrift und ihre Verdeutschung* (Berlin: Schocken Verlag, 1936), pp. 135-137. The English translation of this quotation is from Fox, *In the Beginning,* p. 146.

[7] Nahum Glatzer, introduction to Fox, *In the Beginning,* p. 5.

[8] This and subsequent quotations from Scholem's text are from 'At the Completion of Buber's Translation of the Bible,' trans. Michael A. Meyer, in *The Messianic Idea in Judaism* (New York: Schocken, 1971), pp. 315-319.

For whom is this translation now intended and whom will it influence? ... The Jews for whom you translated are no more. Their children, who have escaped from this horror, will no longer read German. The German language itself has profoundly changed in this generation, as everyone knows who in recent years has had contact with the new German language. And it has not developed in the direction of that language utopia to which your endeavor bears such impressive witness. The contrast between the common language of 1925 and your translation has not decreased in the last thirty-five years; it has become greater.

The nobility of Buber's and Rosenzweig's purpose, coupled with the tragic sequence of events which made impossible the fulfillment of that purpose, inhibit my desire to criticize their work. Nevertheless, I think it important to clarify the principles behind their translation and to distinguish them from my own.

I share with Buber and Rosenzweig the conviction that the text was originally spoken rather than written. The common Hebrew word for Bible, *miqra*, means not scripture, but 'calling out.' And I believe, as Buber and Rosenzweig did, that translations, too, ought to be designed to be read aloud. However, unlike Buber and Rosenzweig, I do not believe that Bible translations ought somehow to sound like the original. Rather, I think translations are more likely to be spoken aloud when they are written unselfconsciously, in the natural rhythms of their own language.

Scholem remarked to Buber in his speech, 'It is a unique feature of your translation that it uses every means to force the reader to read the text aloud.' But one wonders *which* text. Perhaps the most revealing remark in Scholem's letter is that the Buber-Rosenzweig translation 'was an appeal to the reader: Go and learn Hebrew!' I think it is this that comes closest to the truth; the Buber-Rosenzweig translation does not, finally, stand on its own as German literature but performs instead a very different service for the original. By approximating the rhythmic patterns of the Hebrew language, it seeks to engage the curiosity of non-Hebrew readers, enough perhaps to make them want to discover the actual sound of the original. Precisely by failing to satisfy the German literary sensibility, it whets the reader's appetite to learn Hebrew. It is, in this sense, a noble enterprise whose ultimate purpose is to make itself unnecessary.

My translation has no such aims. My intentions were not to return the reader to Hebrew, but to open the text as much as possible to as wide an English-speaking audience as I might reach. My translation is not primarily for Hebrew readers or potential Hebrew readers, but for the many people who cannot make the Hebrew language their own. For those readers I offer the best verse I can write, as faithful as I can make it to my understanding of the original text and to my feeling for it.

*   *   *

The discussions in the ensuing chapters reveal, I hope, the bases of my various departures from the literal and the several principles of fidelity to which I have adhered. Here, I would like to add a few words about the forms and styles of my renditions.

A glance at the thirty-one poems in my version reveals a variety of verse forms: some poems are in couplets with off-rhymes, some in iambic quatrains, some in longer accentual lines, some in short unmetered verse, and so on. This variety is intended to reflect my view of the text as a collection of individual poems, each with its own shape on the page. At the same time, I saw some poems as related, sharing similar speakers, moods, or themes, and I tried to echo these continuities by repeating certain forms. For example, poems 8, 13, and 25, each in the mode of wishing, spoken by a woman, and concluding with the adjuration-refrain, are all rendered in accentual couplets.

I tried for a similar balance with style. I intended the style of the poems to be unified enough to reflect the Song's lyrical eroticism, yet varied enough to express different attitudes and voices, and to guard the repeated material in the text from monotony.

To achieve these formal and stylistic balances between continuity and variation, I sought models in the English and American literary streams, from William Carlos Williams and Theodore Roethke, modern masters of free verse, to the sixteenth- and seventeenth-century poets of England, artisans of meter and rhyme. To these writers I owe a great debt, the debt of tradition; above all, however, I owe these translations to their origin, the place where the journey began.

TWO

THE LITERARY STRUCTURE OF THE SONG

PROBABLY NO BOOK in the Hebrew Bible has been the subject of more controversy concerning its literary classification than the Song of Songs. I do not intend to treat in any depth the long history of interpretation of the Song; the Bible scholar H. H. Rowley has barely summarized the issue in forty-nine heavily footnoted pages,[1] and more recently, Marvin H. Pope has taken up the matter in the lengthy introduction to his translation work for the Anchor Bible series.[2] Pope covers every aspect of the history of the Song's interpretation, from the earliest Jewish and Christian allegorizations to contemporary feminist perspectives, including along the way psychoanalytic, melodramatic, cultic, and mystical approaches.[3] It is clearly beyond my scope to evaluate the theories outlined by Rowley or Pope; moreover, these theories do not bear equally on the literary questions which are the chief concern of this study. For example, some interpretations emphasize original life setting (*Sitz im Leben*), while others are primarily interested in the religious significance of the text. In this chapter I will consider the major positions only as they are relevant to the literary structure of the Song; then I will explain my reconstruction of the text as a collection of thirty-one poems.

The major interpretations view the Song as:

a) an allegory of love between God and the people of Israel (the

[1] 'The Interpretation of the Song of Songs' in *The Servant of the Lord*, 2nd ed. (Oxford: Basil Blackwell, 1965), pp. 197-245.

[2] *The Song of Songs: A New Translation with Introduction and Commentary* (New York: Doubleday, 1977), pp. 89-229.

[3] Idiosyncratically, Pope concludes his survey with several pages on funeral rites, a relatively unexplored area which he believes is 'capable of explaining the Canticles better than any other and is able to subsume aspects of other modes of interpretation as enfolding elements of truth' (p. 229).

Jewish allegorical interpretation), or between Christ and the church or the individual soul (the Christian allegorical interpretation);

b) a drama having two main characters, Solomon and the Shulammite, or three main characters, Solomon and two country lovers;

c) a liturgy, the residue of an ancient fertility cult;

d) a cycle of wedding songs, similar to Syrian marriage songs;

e) a structurally unified secular love poem;

f) a collection or anthology of love poems.

Of these interpretations, the first usually implies narrative structure, at least to the extent that it assumes plot development and posits fixed personae for the voices. But neither plot nor fixed personae are obvious in the text, which does not name any of its speakers. (Solomon is not one of the Song's speakers; the mention of his name in the title and elsewhere is discussed in subsequent chapters.) As we shall see when we analyze the Song's speakers in the next chapter, there seem to be many different voices speaking, not just the two or three main characters implied by allegorical interpretation. Moreover, the Song, unlike, for example, Isaiah 5, does not itself claim to be an allegory and nowhere offers a key to allegorical explication. Although often rich with imaginative insight, the allegorical interpretations do not carry weight among scholars outside the religious world today.

The dramatic view of the Song must also be dismissed on structural grounds. I know of no dramatic interpretation that has not distorted the Song considerably, usually by assuming a *dramatis personae* and scenarios not provided in the text itself, and sometimes by rearranging lines and whole passages.[4] The Song as we have it simply does not conform to dramatic structure, despite the fact that it is composed of monologues and dialogues and seems to have a chorus which interjects from time to time. The presence of monologues, dialogues, and choruses is insufficient basis on which to posit drama, for drama, like narrative, implies plot and the unified portrayal of character.

The view of the Song as the liturgy of an ancient fertility cult does not necessarily imply plot but it does suggest fixed personae in a fixed context; so too the theory of the Song as a cycle of wedding poems,

---

[4] A typical example is Leroy Waterman, *The Song of Songs: Translated and Interpreted as a Dramatic Poem* (Ann Arbor: Univ. of Michigan Press, 1948). Among other things, Waterman transposes 3:6-4:6 to follow 1:1 in order to make his theory of the plot fit the text.

which assumes the main speakers are the bride, groom, and guests in the context of a marriage celebration. Both these overviews, which are the source of a range of theories by nineteenth-and twentieth-century scholars, are based on rather elaborate postulations about the Song's life setting and relationship to other ancient Near Eastern cultures. While these theories may account for some of the material in the Song, or at least for some of its influences, they do not explain the Song as a whole; rather, they impose awkward superstructures which are finally no more convincing than the allegorical or dramatic overviews. Moreover, they deny the obvious content of the Song, which is not primarily concerned with ritual or marriage but with the various emotions of erotic love.

The main objection to the four overviews outlined so far[5] is their imposition of fixed personae and either plot or contextual unity on a text which seems instead to present a variety of voices speaking in a range of settings and in no particular sequence. Thus, the allegorical, dramatic, liturgical, and marriage frameworks all force the variegated material of the Song into confining molds which do not allow it to resonate. Recently, however, there have been other attempts to demonstrate structural unity in the Song without presupposing any of these frameworks, and these demand a closer look here. These analyses read the Song as a secular love poem with internal unity, although each finds a different internal arrangement. The best, I believe, is J. Cheryl Exum's 'A Literary and Structural Analysis of the Song of Songs,'[6] which builds its claim on sophisticated literary observations.

Exum states her purpose to be a 'formal analysis,' noting that, 'Although most commentators make observations regarding the structure or arrangement of the Song, they have given insufficient

___

[5] For the general reader, here is a brief synopsis of the history of these four interpretations: The allegorical and dramatic interpretations of the Song have very early origins, the former dating back at least as far as the early Rabbinic period, first century C.E., and the latter to Origen in the third century C.E. The dramatic view gained currency in the nineteenth century, particularly among German scholars such as Delitzsch, Ewald, and Jacobi, and French scholars such as Renan. It was also in the nineteenth century that the wedding-cycle interpretation came to light, as expounded by Renan, Wetzstein, Budde, and Siegfried. The liturgical view of the Song is a twentieth-century development and may be seen as a modern return to religious interpretation. Its major proponents have been Meek and Wittekindt; Pope's theory may also be considered an offshoot of this view.

attention to the stylistic and rhetorical devices of the poet which comprise and elucidate the overall structure.' She goes on to treat the Song as three pairs of poems (2:7-3:5 and 5:2-6:3; 3:6-5:1 and 6:4-8:3; 1:2-2:6 and 8:4-14), examining the parallels among them. She proposes that the discovery of structural parallels yields the following conclusions: 'Unity of authorship with an intentional design, and a sophistication of poetic style.'

I am not primarily concerned with Exum's first conclusion, 'unity of authorship,' but rather with the point that leads her to it, namely, the structural unity of the text. Her deduction of 'either a single author or a school of poets working closely together' would seem reasonable given the demonstration of structural unity in the text, although we should also allow for the possibility that this unity was imposed by a later compiler. In any case, Exum does not really argue for unity of authorship except insofar as she demonstrates the unity of the text, and it is this argument which I will address. With her second conclusion, 'sophistication of poetic style,' I am in basic agreement. Indeed, I question why she links this to her first conclusion, when the one is in no way dependent on the other.

Exum's analysis rests on her division of the text into three structurally parallel pairs of poems. These structural parallels, she claims, account for various repeated words and phrases in the text, including refrains, and certain recurrent motifs, such as 'seeking and finding.' But structural parallels are not necessary to account for the presence of these repetitions; they can also be explained by viewing the text as a collection of separate poems derived from a common cultural source. For example, the repeated images in the Song may be conventional literary stock, much as Petrarchan imagery was the stock of Renaissance poets. Another consideration is the likely possibility, to which I subscribe, that the Song was originally oral literature, that is, orally composed and transmitted. Oral composition accounts not only

---

[6] *Zeitschrift für die alttestamentliche Wissenschaft*, 85 (1973), 47-79. All quotations from Exum in this chapter are from this article. Other recent attempts to demonstrate structural unity in the Song are: Francis Landy, 'Beauty and the Enigma: An Inquiry into Some Interrelated Episodes of the Song of Songs,' *Journal for the Study of the Old Testament*, 17 (1980), 55-106, and Edwin C. Webster, 'Patterns in the Song of Songs,' *Journal for the Study of the Old Testament*, 22 (1982), 73-93. Also, Phyllis Trible offers an analysis of the Song 'in five major movements of varying lengths' as part of a larger feminist reading of the Song's themes and motifs in *God and the Rhetoric of Sexuality* (Philadelphia: Fortress Press, 1978), chapter 5.

for recurrent themes and motifs, but for the exact duplication of specific phrases and lines. The appearance of catchwords that appear in separate, editorially juxtaposed poems, and the presence of formulaic pairs like 'gold and silver' are further evidence of an oral tradition.[7]

But Exum does more than note the presence of repeated material in the Song; she argues for 'intentional design,' or the specific arrangement of recurrent motifs and phrases. In so doing, she shows some interesting parallels among the poetic units *as she divides them*. Explaining her methodology, she says, 'The criteria used to determine the limits of poems are the repetition of key phrases, words, and motifs, and the contextual coherence of the poems. Sometimes the limits of a poem are not apparent and we must rely on its parallel as a guide.' Although her method here may sometimes seem circular, she is not alone in this, since most analyses of the Song seem to postulate first and then support the postulation with what evidence can be found. The more serious limitation here is that, in the search for parallel poems, Exum overlooks literary features not relevant to her analysis and thus fails to recognize smaller boundaries within the large poems she delineates. She pays little attention, for example, to changes in setting, argument, tone of voice, and speaker-audience relationship, all of which strongly suggest the presence of smaller compositional units.

Exum's argument for linking these smaller units into larger poems is based on the specific placement of certain 'key phrases, words, and motifs.' But these juxtapositions may well be accounted for by the principles of oral composition already mentioned. As Franz Landsberger explains:

We may assume that a compiler who puts into one collection poems which had hitherto circulated by way of mouth, would write them down according to the principle of association. Writing down one poem he would remember and write down another with a similar key word.[8]

Thus, the 'design' of the Song may be the result of skillful compilation of many short poems rather than original structural

[7] For analyses of the features of Biblical poetry which relate to oral composition, see Perry Yoder, 'A-B Pairs and Oral Composition in Hebrew Poetry,' *Vetus Testamentum*, 21 (1971), 470-489, and Robert C. Culley, *Oral Formulaic Language in the Biblical Psalms* (Toronto: Univ. of Toronto Press, 1967).

[8] 'Poetic Units within the Song of Songs,' *Journal of Biblical Literature*, 73 (1954), 204. Landsberger calls this phenomenon 'juxtaposition of key words.' He uses the phrase 'key word' in the sense that is usually referred to in studies of oral literature by the term 'catchword.'

unity. It seems, moreover, that the search for structural unity necessitates a less sensitive reading of many subtle variations within the text. As I see it, the Song opens up most fully when viewed as a collection of several short poems.

Before presenting this last view and then explaining my own division of the text into smaller poems, I want to clarify at least one important reason why the Song's structure is the subject of so much debate. In the earliest exemplar of the Masoretic text (the Leningrad MS., 1008 C.E.),[9] we find the Song divided into chapters and smaller portions designed for reading in synagogues. Also indicated are *p^esuqim*, which are units roughly equivalent to sentences but not necessarily poetic lines; these are what are called Biblical 'verses' in English. The Masoretic accent marks indicate caesuras within the *p^esuqim* as well as conjunctive and disjunctive connections between words; other than that, there is nothing that might be considered punctuation. Poetic units are not apparent: no demarcation is given for individual poems, stanzas, or lines of verse. In other words, the text looks like a mass of prose on the page, divided only into sections and subsections of approximately equal length. Theoretically, then, the Song might be *seen* as having no poetic structure at all; it is therefore easy to understand why its structure has been the subject of such a wide range of speculation.

Yet no one disagrees that the Song *is* poetry, not prose. This is because of its *audibly* apparent rhythms (the coincidence of syntactic units with breath units) and its style (the heavy use of sound plays such as puns and alliterations, and, above all, the reliance upon parallelisms to convey rhythmic units as well as syntactic-semantic structure). A minimal definition of verse, as opposed to prose, might be that it is language in lines. In written verse, lines take a visual shape on the

---

[9] The historical stages of the Song prior to this date are not totally agreed upon. Here is a rough historical outline: Scholars argue the date of composition any time from 950 to 200 B.C.E., and many believe that the poems were composed by several authors over a period of time. Compilation took place some time after composition, in the post-Exilic period, roughly between 500 and 200 B.C.E. The consonantal text was finally fixed and standardized by the time of canonization, i.e., no later than the second century C.E. Between the fourth and seventh centuries C.E., the Masoretes added the vowels and accent marks, indicating how the text was to be recited and where the basic syntactic units were marked off. The Masoretic text is today considered the authoritative Hebrew edition and is used by most interpreters of the Song.

page, with stanza breaks usually indicating longer pauses. Line breaks and stanza breaks in written verse are, in effect, visual indications of how a poem is to be heard. Yet in the case of the Song the matter is reversed: because the original line and stanza divisions are not preserved for us, we must postulate, on the basis of what we can hear from reading the text aloud, where divisions might have been had the text been transcribed as it was heard in its own time.

Now while there is no definitive theory of Hebrew prosody, scholars agree in general about where the poetic lines exist. This is because the Hebrew lines articulate themselves naturally in short breath units of two, three, four, or, very rarely, five beats, these units generally coinciding with syntactic units such as phrases or clauses (enjambement is rare). Thus the division of the text into lines was for me the first and least problematic step in the reconstruction of the text as a poetic document.

Stanza breaks, a matter of considerably less importance and more speculation, came much later. My division of the Hebrew text into stanzas was, in fact, intended less as a reconstruction than as a guide to interpretation. My stanza breaks usually indicate one or more of the following: a change of speaker within a poem, a change of audience, a pause to allow time to pass, a pause to allow for closure and reopening of an extended theme. Sometimes the stanza divisions set off discrete metaphorical units, as in the *wasfs*. In essence, my stanza divisions offer the reader suggestions for reading the text aloud and a guide to hearing its meaning, but they are *not* meant to represent the way the original might have been transcribed in its own time, for we cannot be certain that the concept of stanzas applied to ancient Hebrew verse.

On the other hand, my division of the text into thirty-one poems *is* intended as such a postulation. The presentation of the Song in the Leningrad MS. demonstrates why it is not unreasonable to believe that it is, in fact, a collection of poems rather than a single unified poem. If we assume line units where they are not visually indicated, there is no reason to exclude the possibility of poem units. The view of the text as a collection of several poems is shared by many scholars.[10]

[10] See Robert H. Pfeiffer, *Introduction to the Old Testament*, 2nd ed. (New York: Harper & Brothers, 1948), pp. 708 ff., where a partial list of those in accord with the view of the Song as a collection is given. This is Pfeiffer's own view as well. See also Landsberger, p. 203, where some of the more recent exponents of this position are cited. Landsberger states his concurrence with those 'who see in the Song of Songs, as it is extant, not a connected whole but a

Robert Gordis, in the introduction to his translation of the Song, traces this view back five centuries: 'If the Song of Songs be approached without any preconception, it reveals itself as a collection of lyrics. This view of the book was taken by a Middle High German version of the 15th century, which divided it into 54 songs.'[11]

The reasons for viewing the Song as a collection are many. Gordis notes 'the wide gamut of its emotions'; we might add to this the several distinct settings, the range of situations and subject matter, and the considerable variety of tones and moods. The strongest argument, however, is the presence of many different speakers, addressing different audiences. In the next chapter I analyze the various relationships between speakers and audiences in the Song and attempt to demonstrate, on the basis of this analysis, the presence of several different types of lyric poems in the collection.

Of the interpreters who view the text as a collection and divide it as such, however, no two agree exactly on the divisions. Gordis divides the text into twenty-eight poems, but notes that 'Jastrow and Budde each finds 23 songs . . . Haller finds 26, Bettan 18.' Gordis also allows that, in his presentation, several of the poems are fragmentary and some may be doublets. The fact that scholars differ in their division of the text does not undermine the belief that the Song is not a unity. As Gordis explains:

> The division of the songs will depend upon the changes in theme, viewpoint, background or form. These criteria will not always be sufficiently exact to command universal assent. Much will be dependent upon the literary taste and insight, as well as upon the knowledge, of the interpreter. But this is simply a restatement of the truth that exegesis is essentially an art, which rests upon a foundation of scientific knowledge.

For my own division of the text into thirty-one poems, it was the perception of content that guided the delineation of form. Besides the various shifts in the text which indicated the end of one poem and the beginning of the next, the presence of self-contained arguments also

collection of several poems.' Most recently, Roland Murphy ('Towards a Commentary on the Song of Songs,' *Catholic Biblical Quarterly*, 39 [1977], 482-496) has argued that 'The Song is a collection of love poems that have been given a certain unity by means of a dialogue pattern, and by the use of catchwords and repetitions.' Murphy notes that the view of the Song as a collection 'seems to be growing.'

11 *The Song of Songs* (New York: Jewish Theological Seminary of America, 1961), pp. 16-17. Further quotations from Gordis in this chapter are from pp. 17-18 of his book.

suggested the limits of poem units. For the most part, I found that individual poems had internal coherence and were not mere fragments.

For example, 1:2-4 of the Hebrew is a passage praising the beloved and inviting lovemaking, spoken by a woman to a man whom she compares to a king. The unit seems to close naturally with the repetition of the words 'they love you.' The next verse in the Hebrew brings us into a new context. A woman speaks, but her audience is not the city women and her tone of voice is defiant. This passage, 1:5-6, is a monologue of self-assertion; it does not appear to be a continuation of the previous speech. On the basis of these observations, I treat 1:2-4 and 1:5-6 as two separate poems.

There are, of course, instances where the divisions between poems are not so readily apparent. For example, poems 16 and 17 in my reconstruction of the text are both invitations spoken by a man to his beloved, whom he calls 'bride.' Other similarities between these poems are the speakers' urgent tones and the references to Lebanon. One might therefore see 16 and 17 as a single poem, but I saw sufficient reason to separate them. Whereas in poem 16 Lebanon is a dangerous place, the habitat of wild animals, in 17 it is associated with pleasant fragrance, like that of the beloved's clothing. The mood of 17 is gentler than that of 16 because its context is less threatening. The appearance of the words 'bride' and 'Lebanon' in both poems may be the result of an editorial juxtaposition; in other words, they may be the catchwords which led a compiler to place the poems alongside one another.[12] Finally, each poem makes a complete and separate argument: in 16, the woman is urged to leave her dangerous abode and join her lover; in 17, the speaker describes, from near rather than far, the power of his beloved to excite him with her beauty and sensuality. Thus, while it is conceivable that the two poems may have been one, it benefits each to be read and heard separately.

We have seen how, in oral literature like the Song, content may suggest ways to delineate structure when structure is otherwise ambiguous. So too our perception of structure in the Song influences how we read its content. In the next chapter I will explore the internal structure of the Song — the types of poems it comprises — as groundwork for further inquiry into its meaning.

[12] This is an example of the principle referred to above by Landsberger, who applies the same principle to separate 1:5 from 1:6. He argues that these are not a single poem but two distinct poems juxtaposed because the word 'black' appears in both; I treat 1:5-6 as a single poem.

THREE

TYPES OF LOVE LYRIC IN THE SONG

IF THE SONG is not a structural unity, what kind of compilation is it? I maintain that it is a collection — specifically, a collection of lyric love poems. But what exactly do we mean by 'lyric'? The terms 'lyric' and 'lyrical' are surely among the more impressionistic words in our language; we seem to use them as much to characterize and praise as to specifiy and distinguish. Yet we do have certain things in mind when we call a work 'lyrical,' and it may be worth exploring both the more apparent and the less obvious senses of the term in order to see how they apply to the Song.

If lyric verse is distinguished from narrative and dramatic verse primarily by length and scope, all the poems in the Song would have to be seen as lyrics. So too, if we think of the lyric as sensual, the exquisitely rich imagery of the Song would certainly qualify the Song as lyrical poetry.

Indeed, the Song fits even the etymological definition, which proclaims the lyric to be musical or song-like. A lyric — from the Greek *lura*, lyre — was originally a poem meant to be sung to musical accompaniment. Probably no other ancient text, at least in the Western tradition, has been more often or more variously chanted, sung, or set to music. In this regard, the very title of the book — *sir hassirim*, 'the Song of Songs' — is revealing. The relationship between poetry and song was undoubtedly a close one for the ancient Hebrews and is very likely related to the oral tradition from which the Song of Songs derives. Even beyond the time of its composition and compilation, the Song continued to be orally transmitted by the Jews, who chanted it in synagogues and homes, in Ashkenazic communities on the Sabbath of Passover and in Sephardic communities on the eve of every Sabbath. The Masoretic accent marks were used as notations for the various cantillations that developed, many of which have been preserved to the present day. In addition to being ritually chanted, the words of the Song have been often set to music and continue to be set today, attesting to the Song's musicality, and reconfirming its place in Hebrew oral culture. Indeed, if 'lyric' means 'songlike,' then the Song of Songs is an archetypal lyric collection.

Brevity, sensuality, and musicality, however, do not suffice to define the lyric. The lyric tends to be a subjective form, expressive of *personal* feeling toward specific subject matter and addressed to a *particular* listener. The speaker of the lyric is usually an individual I-speaker, although, as we shall see shortly, more than one voice may sometimes speak a lyric. The subject matter of the lyric can vary widely: it may be simple or complex, commonplace or extraordinary, secular or religious, public or private. And the audience of the lyric (by which I mean the listener whom the speaker addresses, not necessarily the readership of the poem) may be almost anyone — a relation, a friend, a beloved, a stranger, God, or the self. To see what kinds of lyric comprise the Song, it is useful to examine the Song's various speakers in relation to their subject matter and audience.

For example, in the various poems of the Song in which a lover speaks to or about a beloved,[1] there is present, to use Martin Buber's phrase, an I-Thou relationship.[2] This relationship is most evident when the speaker directly addresses the beloved, but it may still be felt when the beloved is spoken of only in the third person. In other kinds of poem in the Song, however — those whose subject matter is erotic but which do not focus primarily on the beloved or the personal love relationship — the I-Thou relationship may be subordinate or absent. The presence or absence, and relative prominence, of the I-Thou relationship may therefore provide a means of distinguishing different types of love lyric in the Song.

Before applying these concepts to the Song, I want to establish two basic categories of poems: monologues and dialogues. For the purpose of this discussion, monologues refer to poems having no change of speaker within them, whether spoken by a single voice or by a group.

[1] Throughout this study, I use the word 'beloved' to refer to the loved one, as opposed to 'lover,' which designates the speaker or initiator. Obviously, men and women can, and do, play either role in the poems.

[2] Buber uses the phrase 'I-Thou' to refer to primary, mutual relationship, distinguishing it from 'I-It,' which is subject-object experience. Martin Buber, *I and Thou*, trans. Walter Kaufmann (New York: Charles Scribner's Sons, 1970), pp. 53-85.

Dialogues refer to poems in which conversation takes place between speakers or groups of speakers. (I do not imply by these terms any association with the genre of drama).

The following, then, are six types of lyrics which can be distinguished in the Song:

a) the 'love monologue' — a poem spoken by an I-speaker to and/or about a beloved, in which the beloved is the implicit audience, whether or not s/he is also the explicit audience (poems 1, 4, 5, 8, 10, 12, 13, 15, 16, 17, 20, 21 [symbolic], 23, 24, 25, 27, and 28);

b) the 'love dialogue' — a conversation between two lovers (poems 3, 6, 7, 9, 18, and 31);

c) a monologue spoken by an I-speaker in a love relationship, to an audience outside that relationship (poems 2 and 30);

d) a monologue spoken by an unidentifiable speaker (probably a group of speakers) to an unspecified audience, about erotic subject matter, either direct or symbolic (poems 11, 14, and 26);

e) a dialogue between an I-speaker and a group of speakers, about erotic subject matter (poems 22 and 29);

f) the composite poem (19).

Because of its greater length, and especially because of its complex structure, which suggests narrative and even dramatic features, 19 seems to conform least to our emerging definition of the lyric. Nevertheless, poem 19 bears important similarity to the poems of type (a), because its frame is the dream-speech of a single speaker, and only within this frame do other speeches occur. Thus, although it comprises both monologues and dialogues, 19 suggests itself as a single poetic unit, essentially lyric in expression, within which narrative and dramatic elements play. I treat is as a sixth type — a composite poem — and examine its structure in depth below.

a) Love monologues— poems in which a single speaker, male or female, speaks to or about a beloved — comprise over half the poems in the Song. Often in the love monologues, the beloved is directly addressed, and therefore is the *explicit* audience of the speech. Even when the beloved is not directly addressed, however, we might say that s/he remains the *implicit* audience because s/he is the real focus of the speaker's feelings. Thus, the love monologue may sometimes have a double audience: an apparent (explicit) audience such as a group of outsiders, and the real (implicit) hearer, who is always the beloved.

Double audiences are found more frequently in love monologues spoken by females than in those by males. Of the love monologues spoken by a woman — poems 1, 5, 8, 12, 13, 24, 25, 27, and 28 — all but 27 and 28 refer in part if not entirely to the beloved as 'he,' thus implying another audience besides him.[3] Often, as in all or parts of 5, 8, 12, 13, and 24, the speaker seems to be addressing herself — wishing, anticipating, or daydreaming — as in a fantasy. In poems 8, 13, and 25, she explicitly addresses another audience, the 'women of the city.' In all these poems, however, the focus of feeling remains the beloved; he is the implicit audience of all these speeches. In 13, the speaker cannot address her beloved explicitly because he is absent, but the longing she expresses can be satisfied only by him. In 8, the food she requests, ostensibly from the city women (the Hebrew imperatives are directed to a plural 'you'), is a metaphor for erotic attention, which only the beloved can provide. He is, throughout, the cause and focus of her feelings; only his embrace will cure her lovesickness.

Thus the I-Thou relationship is strongly implied in all the love monologues spoken by women, even those ostensibly addressed to people other than the beloved. Its presence may seem more obvious, however, in the love monologues spoken by men — poems 4, 10, 15, 16, 17, 20, 21, and 23 — because of these, all but 21 *explicitly* address the beloved. The male speakers of love monologues, unlike the females, never address a specified group of outsiders such as the city women, and only twice — in poems 21 and 23 — do they address themselves.[4]

Because male speakers in the Song rarely fantasize or address outsiders, and more frequently than women address the beloved explicitly, one might conjecture that males were allowed more forthrightness than females in Biblical culture. Perhaps, as one scholar has speculated in personal correspondence, the fact that wishing,

[3] This is not apparent in the English version of poem 1 where, in order to avoid confusion, I changed the third-person pronoun to the second person. See the note to poem 1 in chapter six for further explanation.

[4] In poem 21, we cannot even be certain of this much: both speaker and audience are difficult to determine because, although the Hebrew grammar indicates a single I-speaker, it does not specify gender. Nevertheless, we may deduce a male speaker from the content: elsewhere in the Song, the garden setting — 'orchard' in my translation — represents female sexuality, as do the images of vines and pomegranates. This small spring song seems to be a self-addressed male fantasy — a veiled description of an anticipated union with the beloved. The mode of fantasy seems also to dominate poem 23, which is addressed partly to the beloved and partly to the self. The word $w^e yih^e yu$-na' (line 7 of the Hebrew) grammatically indicates this mode with the particle suffix na', implying wish.

imagining, and fantasizing is largely confined to women speakers 'may reflect women's social dependence in that ancient society, as (traditionally) in ours. It is men who are permitted the social *initiatives* in love and marriage: the custom is that women must wait on men's actions.' Yet the poems spoken by a woman are hardly reserved or shy; they are, rather, uninhibited and outspoken. One might on the other hand speculate that women in ancient Hebrew society were more self-reflective and socially communicative than men, and thus they more often verbalized their emotions to themselves and to others. We might, if we wished to stretch the point, deduce that they had more highly developed imaginations and richer fantasy lives. Another scholar, Chaim Rabin, in fact proposes that the entire Song may be a woman's fantasy. He notes that the female speaker is the 'chief person in the Song,' and that 'she expresses deep and complicated emotions,' compared to those expressed by the male. Rabin continues, 'it is surely significant that there are a number of occasions when he speaks in her imagination, but never she in his . . . . A case could be made out for the theory that everything the lover says is imagined by her, even if this is not expressly stated.'[5]

Whether or not one is convinced by Rabin's provocative proposal, the love monologues of both men and women seem to be the purest form of lyric expression in the Song, because each is the intensely personal speech of a single I speaker, whose real audience is a single hearer, the beloved Thou.

b) Love dialogues are poems in which two lovers speak to each other with invitations, mutual praise, or questions and replies. Because the two voices are I-speakers, each expressing personal feeling to and about the other, we may consider these dialogues variations of the love lyric, even though the lyric is usually thought of as the speech of a single voice. Poems 3, 6, 7, 9, 18, and 31 are all examples of this type, although poem 9 is, strictly, a monologue within a monologue. (Poem 9 is a woman's speech, in which she records the speech of her lover; thus, she refers to him in the third person, but he addresses her in the second person. Poem 18 also departs slightly from the dialogue form; it concludes with the interjection of a third voice addressing the lovers.)

The love dialogues share several characteristics, including playful or expectant tones, and the setting of the domesticated countryside.

---

[5] 'The Song of Songs and Tamil Poetry,' *Studies in Religion*, 3 (1973-74), pp. 205-219.

The most significant feature common to these poems, however, is the sense of intimacy, or reciprocity of emotion, that they express.

The reciprocity of the I-Thou relationship is most obvious in the love dialogues because they are (with the exception of poem 9) direct conversations. Here, not only do the two speakers express mutual feelings for each other; they often use similar metaphors and sometimes identical phrases to describe their appreciation. For example, in poem 7, the man describes his beloved as a flower among brambles; she responds by calling him a fruit tree in the thickets. In poem 6, the woman responds to her lover's exclamation ('How fine / you are') with a similar outburst. In poem 3, the man's response to the woman's question may at first seem evasive; but in fact the tone of *both* voices is coy: they seem to be participating in a lovers' game of hide-and-seek. Similarly, the woman's reply to her lover in poem 31 sounds like a rejection ('go now'), but as we will see later (in chapter five), it is actually a veiled invitation to return later.

Because the feeling of reciprocity is central to these dialogues, I have tried to emphasize this in the translations by rhythmically and tonally balancing voices within poems. For example, poem 7 is in iambic quatrains, each closing with the word 'love.' The refrain of 'love' is a departure from the Hebrew, introduced to emphasize the parallel feelings of the two speakers. Another example is poem 31, where each speaker has the same number of lines, divided into similar rhythmic units.

Because two voices speak in the love dialogues, these poems depart from the traditional conception of lyric form; but as love poems they express perhaps most perfectly the mutuality of I-Thou love.

c) Poems 2 and 30 are monologues spoken by an I-speaker, but not to a beloved, and only symbolically and secondarily about a beloved; in neither poem is the beloved felt to be the implicit audience. Although erotic relationships are alluded to in both poems (the vines and vineyards are sexual symbols), they are not the focus of the speeches. In poem 2, a woman addresses an audience of city women, that is, people outside any intimate love relationship. Similarly in poem 30, a man addresses first an unspecified audience and then King Solomon, a figure of power and wealth outside the love relationship. The king is a foil for the speaker, whose defiant tone is like that of the speaker in poem 2. Both poems express self-pride more than love for another, and although the self-esteem of the speakers is bolstered by the erotic relationship in the background, the beloved is not nearly as prominent as in the poems of the first two types. The intensity of the speakers' personal feeling towards their subject matter in poems 2 and 30 contributes to the the poems' lyricism, but these poems are far less expressive of I-Thou feeling than the love monologues and love dialogues. I have rendered 2 and 30 in metrical quatrains for formal effect.

d) Poems 11, 14, and 26 are spoken by unidentifiable speakers to an unspecified audience (except for the last stanza of poem 14, which is explicitly addressed to the Jerusalem daughters). These poems refer, either symbolically (the vines) or directly, to erotic relationships, but they are spoken by outside observers rather than participants. While their mood is animated and intense, it is doubtful whether the tone expresses *personal* feeling; although we cannot be certain, it seems that the speakers are not individual I-speakers but groups of voices. In this way these poems are unlike the other monologues in the text and seem to be less lyrical in expression. Because the personae of these poems are unclearly defined, I set the poems in the typeface designating unidentifiable speakers.

e) The dialogue poems 22 and 29 differ from the love dialogues in that neither of them is a conversation between an I and a Thou; rather, the dialogue takes place between an individual and a group of speakers. In poem 22, the I-speaker is barely prominent; the poem is dominated by the voices of those addressing and praising her, who seem to be a chorus of men. Thus in tone and feeling, 22 most resembles poem 14 (type d), where a chorus of voices (here probably women) describes the beauty of the marriage procession. In poem 29, a young sister replies to her protective older brothers with a tone of self-pride similar to that of the speakers of poems 2 and 30 (type c). Although the subject matter of both 22 and 29 is erotic, I-Thou love is not the primary focus of either of the poems. I have rendered poems 22 and 29, like 14, 2 and 30, with metrical forms.

f) Poem 19, comprising about an eighth of the entire Song, includes the voices of several speakers and explicitly addresses several different audiences: the self, the beloved, the city women. It is set in a variety of contexts, shifting from the bedroom to the city streets and finally to the garden. It spans a wide range of moods, and seems even to have dramatic development, including climax and denouement. But its frame, as we have already noted, is that of a love monologue spoken by an I-speaker, whose beloved is the implied audience.

The poem begins with the statement of a woman who claims to be asleep. It is thus the only self-proclaimed dream poem in the collection, although, as we have seen, the dreamlike modes of wishing, anticipating, and daydreaming appear in several other poems. Relating her dream to an unspecified audience, possibly herself, the speaker records the voice of her lover at the door. Thus far the poem is a monologue within a monologue, similar in structure to poem 9. But now the woman responds to her lover's invitation, explicitly addressing herself: 'Should I get up, get dressed, and dirty my feet?' After this, the poem turns to narrative, as the speaker describes a sequence which takes her from her bed to the door and finally into the city streets in search of her beloved. At some point during the narrative, the distinction between dream and waking life becomes blurred; it is unclear whether subsequent events happen within the speaker's dream or whether she is now awake.

In the narration is an encounter with the city guards: 'The men who roam the streets, / guarding the walls, / beat me and tear away my robes.' Following this moment of violence, which is unmatched in the Song, the speaker turns away from the narrative and appeals directly to the city women for help in finding her beloved. A dialogue then follows, in which the skeptical women ask the distraught speaker who her beloved is, and she reponds with a lengthy description of him in a *wasf* (the *wasf* is discussed in the next chapter). The *wasf* here constitutes a love monologue, similar to the one spoken by a male in poem 15, but here the beloved is referred to throughout in the third person. The closing lines of the *wasf* affirm the mutuality of the I-Thou relationship and climax the poem. The poem concludes with a short dialogue between the woman and the city women, who have been the explicit audience of this *wasf*. Convinced by her description of her beloved, they are eager to help her find him; but she has apparently calmed herself and no longer wants their help. She tells them that her beloved is in 'his garden' (with her) and that the love relationship is intact. Thus, in the closing stanzas of the poem, the woman reaffirms the I-Thou relationship and excludes her explicit audience, the city women, from participation in it. The poem ends on a note of intimacy: anticipated reunion with the beloved.

The biggest challenge in translating this poem was finding a form which would contain its various sections and, at the same time, reveal similarities between the individual sections and other poems in the collection. I finally decided on a combination of free verse and metrical forms. I began with free verse lines to introduce the anxious dream-speech and shifted to metrical lines for the dialogue with the city women. I rendered the *waṣf* in iambic quatrains (similar to the treatment of the *waṣf* in poem 22) and repeated the same meter in the concluding two stanzas, to extend the affirmative tone of the *waṣf* into the poem's resolution. Thus, if the English translation of poem 19 looks like a small compilation of even smaller lyrics, it is because I have attempted to highlight its composite form.

This analysis has attempted to reveal similarities and differences among poems in the Song based on the degrees to which they share the features of lyric form and upon the ways in which they express the I-Thou love relationship. We have seen that all the poems deal with aspects of love and eros, and that all may be classified as lyrics. But some poems, those in which the I-Thou relationship is central, seem to be *archetypal* love lyrics, whereas others are variations on the archetype. The collection as a whole emerges as a variegated compilation of several types of love lyric, expressing a wide range of tone and feeling.

FOUR

THE *WAṢF*

IT IS A PARADOX of human nature that strangeness, like its opposite, often breeds contempt. While the Song has been widely celebrated by Bible scholars and lay audiences alike, there is another mood, of uneasiness, even embarrassment, which sometimes murmurs beneath the din of our applause. This discontent seems to surface in discussions of a kind of passage in the Song known to Bible scholars as the *waṣf*. The scholarly investigations and treatments of the *waṣf* reveal some of the serious limitations of Bible scholarship in the realm of literary study, and expose, moreover, some of the prejudices most frequently applied to the Song as a whole. Primarily to shed light on these problems and to suggest solutions, including alternative ways to interpret the content of the Song, I treat the *waṣf* as a separate subject.

Waṣf, an Arabic word meaning 'description,' has come to refer to a kind of poem or poetic fragment that describes through a series of images the parts of the male and female body. While *waṣfs* are not uncommon in modern Arabic poetry, in ancient Hebrew literature they appear only in the Song of Songs. The similarity between certain passages in the Song and modern Arabic poems was discovered in the last century; because of this, the technical term *waṣf* has become familiar in scholarly studies of the Song.

Although the *waṣf* shares stylistic features with the rest of the Song, relying for poetic effect on parallelism, sound play, and the use of short rhythmic lines, it is formally stricter and more predictable than any other material in the collection. Essentially a catalogue which describes in sequence, from top to bottom or bottom to top, segments of the male or female body, the *waṣf* appears, in part or in whole, in several different types of poem in the Song. Poem 15 is a love monologue with a partial *waṣf*; 19 is a composite which contains a complete *waṣf*; 20 is a love monologue which repeats some of the *waṣf*

80

found in 15; and 22, framed as a dialogue, almost entirely comprises a complete *waṣf*. Of these four, the *waṣf*s in poems 15, 20, and 22 are descriptions of a female, while the *waṣf* in 19 describes a male. To this last distinction and related issues I will return later.

Not only is the form of the *waṣf* fairly rigid and its subject matter determined at the outset, its treatment of the subject also follows a pattern: each part of the physique is described by means of specific, often unlikely images drawn from the realms of nature and artifice. While the imagery in the *waṣf* is usually visual, it sometimes appeals to other senses, as in the tactile 'breasts like fawns' or the olfactory and taste-like associations of 'lips like lilies.'

It has been my observation that the imagery in the *waṣf*s is associated by English readers with the 'peculiar' poetic characteristics of the Song and with the 'exotic' nature of ancient Hebrew sensibility. (When giving readings of my translation, I find audiences particularly curious to hear how I rendered those strings of strange images known previously to them through the standard translations.) What is more difficult to understand, however, is the bewilderment of Bible scholars, who read the *waṣf*s in the original Hebrew and are familiar enough with texts of the ancient Near East not to consider ancient Hebrew literature exotic. Here are some typical examples of what these scholars say about the *waṣf*s:

The comparison of the girl's hair to a flock of goats would have been straightforward and legitimate if mention of the slopes of Gilead had been omitted. As the image stands, the mountain background is, in reference to a girl's head, too large for the goats, for if they are bunched together there are too many slopes bare of goats, but if they are scattered the emphasis falls upon the girl's hairs rather than her hair. Thus the figure is bizarre, if not grotesque, possibly by intent of the author.[1]

Only as playful banter can be rationally explained the grotesque description by the lover to the damsel of her neck as 'like the tower of David built for an armoury,' of her nose 'as the tower of Lebanon which looketh toward Damascus,' and of her head like mount Carmel (iv 4, vii 5, 6), and similar comical comparisons of her other limbs.[2]

To our sensibilities the images are admittedly comical and puzzling. Consequently, one must infer either that this was the poet's intention, in which case the *waṣf*s are not 'descriptive love songs' at all but parodies, or that our perspective radically differs from the poet's.[3]

[1] Leroy Waterman, *The Song of Songs: Translated and Interpreted as a Dramatic Poem* (Ann Arbor: Univ. of Michigan Press, 1948), p. 63.

[2] M. H. Segal, 'The Song of Songs,' *Vetus Testamentum*, 12 (1962), 480.

[3] Richard N. Soulen, 'The *Waṣf*s of the Song of Songs and Hermeneutic,' *Journal of Biblical Literature*, 86 (1967), 185.

'Bizarre,' 'grotesque,' 'comical,' 'puzzling' — do these aptly describe the imagery in the Song? If so, what words might describe acclaimed passages in English literature such as the conceits of the metaphysical poets: for example, Crashaw's comparison in 'The Weeper' of Mary Magdalene's tears to 'two faithful fountains; / Two walking baths; two weeping motions; / Portable, and compendious oceans'; or Donne's two lovers like legs of a compass in 'A Valediction: Forbidding Mourning'? And how shall we characterize the poetry of the modern age, including the imagism of writers like Pound, Moore, Williams, H. D.? Will it not seem odd to find poets comparing the inside of a subway station to a branch of a tree, as in Pound's famous two-line poem 'In a Station of the Metro': 'The apparition of these faces in the crowd; / Petals on a wet, black bough.'? And how will we even begin to understand foreign literatures which make poetic statements like this one: 'Inside of one potato / there are mountains and rivers.'?[4]

The point seems obvious: the difficulty resides not in the nature of the *wasfs* but rather in the critical interpretation. The flaw is not in our text but in the failure of scholars to appreciate the very essence of metaphor, at the core of great poetry from many different eras and cultures. That essence is the extensive psychic association which the poet Robert Bly calls 'leaping':

Thought of in terms of language, leaping is the ability to associate fast. In a great ancient or modern poem, the considerable distance between the associations, the distance the spark has to leap, gives the lines their bottomless feeling, their space, and the speed of the association increases the excitement of the poetry.[5]

It is essentially this leap the metaphor makes — the leap between object and the image which describes it, that is, between tenor and vehicle —which troubles Bible scholars. Richard Soulen points out that a fault with scholarly interpretation lies with its literalistic approach.[6] This seems right, especially if we understand literalism here to mean the need to find between tenor and vehicle a one-to-one correspondence in all details. So Waterman, in the passage quoted above, cannot accept the metaphor of hair like a flock of goats on a mountainside because the size of individual hairs in relation to the size

---

[4] 'Potato' by Shinkichi Takahashi, trans. Harold P. Wright, in Robert Bly, *Leaping Poetry* (Boston: Beacon Press, 1975), p. 19.

[5] Bly, p. 4.

[6] This remark and all subsequent quotations from Soulen are from the article cited above, 183-190.

of the head is not exactly in proportion to the relationship of size between goats and a mountain.

At the other extreme, however, Soulen proposes to eliminate all visualizable correspondence between tenor and vehicle, arguing that this is what T. S. Eliot had in mind when he spoke of 'objective correlative.' Soulen writes:

> Its [the *waṣf's*] purpose is not to provide a parallel to visual appearance or, as we shall see, primarily to describe feminine or masculine qualities metaphorically. The *tertium comparationis* must be seen instead in the feelings and sense experiences of the poet himself who then uses a vivid and familiar imagery to present to his hearers knowledge of those feelings in the form of art.

Soulen is right to note that the imagery in the *waṣfs* is vivid and familiar, for certainly it must have been so in the cultural context of its time. But he offers little to make it similarly vivid or familiar to us, since he declines to analyze it in its particulars, either unwilling or unable to find in it *particular* objective correlatives for emotional experience. Rather, he concludes:

> That interpretation is most correct which sees the imagery of the *waṣf* as a means of arousing emotions consonant with those experiences by the suitor as he beholds the fullness of his beloved's attributes . . . Just as the sensual experiences of love, beauty, and joy are vivid but ineffable, so the description which centers in and seeks to convey these very subjective feelings must for that reason be unanalytical and imprecise.

This is hardly a valid application of Eliot's principle, nor is it an accurate description of what poetry does, for it fails to address the question of *how* emotions are aroused in the reader — how, finally, the ineffable ideal is conveyed through words. By reducing the imagery in the *waṣfs* to vague evocation of ineffable feelings, Soulen deprives the relationship between tenor and vehicle of meaning. The point of comparison between a woman's hair and flocks of goats on a mountainside lies, for him, 'simply in the emotional congruity existing between two beautiful yet otherwise disparate sights.' But if this were so, the poet might have chosen any beautiful thing for an image; there would hardly be a point to interpreting this particular metaphor, or any other. Moreover, there would be no way to distinguish an apt metaphor from a poor one, here or in any text, for as long as tenor and vehicle had vaguely similar emotional associations, the metaphor would be valid.

But one expects more of good poetry, and the Song fulfills these expectations. In fact, the metaphors in the Song express a sophisticated poetic sensibility which, although foreign to us today, can be made accessible through critical analysis. The process is simply one of proper visualization — taking the right focus or perspective, making explicit the implicit context, filling in the unverbalized details. Take the image that has so perturbed the scholars: one can easily picture hair to be like goats on a mountainside by viewing the scene from a distance. From afar, the sight of goats winding down the slopes of the Israeli countryside is striking: the dark animals weave a graceful pattern against the paler background of the hills, suggesting dark waves of hair falling down a woman's back. Similarly, a herd of sheep, emerging fresh from the water, provides an ingenious metaphor when seen at a distance: the paired, white animals suggest twin rows of white teeth. If this seems contrived to our sensibilities, we should at least recognize that it is no more so than the Petrarchan convention of comparing teeth to pearls. In fact, most of the images in the *wasfs* are no more difficult to visualize than the more familiar Petrarchan figures of speech found in Renaissance poetry. With probing, even the most abstruse images in the *wasfs* open up to visualization. Take, for example, the forehead behind the veil, which is compared to a slice of pomegranate. It is puzzling only at first; after reflecting on it with the mind's eye, we see a gleam of red seeds through a net of white membrane. Might this not be like ruddy skin glimpsed through a mesh of white veil? Once we see the image, we realize that it is no more artificial nor less artful than the Petrarchan comparison of cheeks to roses.

It is unnecessary and unfortunate to dismiss the images in the *wasf* as either bizarre or imprecise. Meaningful interpretation lies between these extremes, in nonliteralistic visualization. Thus in translating the *wasfs*, when an image depended upon familiarity with a foreign landscape, I sometimes suggested vantage points or settings so that modern English readers would see in it what the original audience might have seen. Where the King James states, 'thy hair is as a flock of goats, that appear from mount Gilead,' I rendered, 'Your hair — as black as goats / winding down the slopes,' hinting at color and contour where they might otherwise be missed. For the same reason I often eliminated proper place names and substituted descriptions, as here in 'the slopes' for 'mount Gilead,' and, in another *wasf,* 'two silent pools' for 'pools in Heshbon,' 'the hills' for 'Damascus,' 'majestic mountain' for 'Carmel.' (See the note to poem 22 in chapter six for further information about these places.) When an image was not primarily visual, I tried to indicate its specific sensory appeal, as in 'Lips like lilies, sweet / And wet with dew.' Occasionally, to keep a metaphor from sounding hackneyed, I introduced a new detail, as in 'Hair in waves of black / Like wings of ravens.' Although wings are not mentioned in the original, neither is it likely that the Hebrew phrase 'black as a raven' was, in its time, the cliché that it has become in English.

Thus the method of interpretative visualization led me often to lines which differ from those in the standard translations. My goal was to let the images be vivid rather than puzzling pictures of a foreign but accessible culture, in hopes that the imagery of the Song might eventually be demystified for both scholarly and general audiences.

* * *

A related literary issue which has been raised specifically in connection with the *waṣf*, but which has ramifications for our understanding of the Song as a whole, is the topic of male and female roles and representations in the Song, and their conformity to stereotypes. One quote from Soulen should help illuminate the serious problems in scholarly interpretation of this question:

The poetic imagination at work in 5:10-16 where the maiden speaks of her lover is less sensuous and imaginative than in the *waṣfs* of chapters 4 and 7. This is due in part to the limited subject matter and may even be due to the difference in erotic imagination between poet and poetess.

Now let us look once more at the text. A brief glance at the *waṣf* in 5:10-16 (my poem 19) reveals that it is no less sensuous and imaginative than any of the other *waṣfs*. Soulen's evaluation, then, perhaps derives from a preconception that the description of a man's body, as opposed to a woman's, is necessarily 'limited subject matter.' Indeed, such a preconception is not surprising in a culture where men are trained to assume that exaltation of male beauty is frivolous at best, embarrassing at worst. With such bias, any attempt to describe or praise the male body is doomed to fail. However, this bias was hardly embedded in the poetic imagination of the original text: there is nothing at all embarrassed or limited about the female voice speaking the *waṣf*. And this voice, of course, may have been created by either a male or female poet. The deduction of a 'poetess' behind a female persona is not only naive but surprising in its context, because Soulen, like most scholars, talks in general about the author of the Song as male.[7] There is a double prejudice at work here. On the one hand Soulen speaks of the poet as masculine throughout the essay, seeming to disregard the possibility that women contributed to the authorship of the text. On the other hand, when faced with a description of male beauty, he assumes that the passage was composed by a female, at which point he dismisses it as inferior and not warranting further study. (The quoted statement comes from a footnote; Soulen never even mentions this *wasf* again in his text.) Finally, he assumes that poets and poetesses have different (levels of? qualities of?) 'erotic imagination.' The imagination of the poetess is, for Soulen, not just 'different' but inferior; it is the possible cause of a less lively poem.

Soulen's attitude toward the text is hardly unique; on the contrary, it is representative of much modern scholarship. But no matter how common this attitude, we should recognize that it derives from specific, culture-bound prejudices which are incompatible with the cultural sensibility that created the Song, a text that offers a thoroughly nonsexist view of heterosexual love. As is apparent in many poems in the Song, women speak as assertively as men, initiating action at least as often; so too, men are free to be as gentle, as vulnerable, and even as coy as women. Men and women are similarly praised by each other for their sensuality and beauty, not only in the *wasfs* but throughout the Song. As another Bible scholar, Phyllis Trible, has eloquently demonstrated, the Song affirms and celebrates mutuality; in it 'there is no male dominance, no female subordination, and no stereotyping of either sex.'[8]

Sexist interpretation of the *wasf*, and of the Song in general, is a striking example of how the text can be distorted by culturally biased

[7] A notable exception to the scholarly assumption that the Song was written by a man or men is S. D. Goitein's 'Nasim Keyosrot Suge Sifrut Bammiqra' ' ('Women as Creators of Types of Literature in the Bible') in *'iyyunim Bammiqra'* (Tel Aviv: Yavneh, 1967), pp. 248-317.

[8] 'Depatriarchalizing in Biblical Interpretation,' *Journal of the American Academy of Religion*, 41 (1973), 45. See pp. 42-45 for the analysis which leads her to this point. To date, at least one male scholar has acknowledged that Trible is right: 'With regard to the Song of Song she is certainly correct in recognizing the equal and even dominant role of the female and the absence of male chauvinism or patriarchalism.' Marvin H. Pope, *The Song of Songs: A New Translation with Introduction and Commentary* (New York: Doubleday, 1977), p. 210. Are we perhaps at the brink of a new era, in which we can celebrate rather than distort the nonsexist character of this and other Biblical texts?

reading. To interpret the Song authentically, we must shed the cultural blinders that make what is foreign seem strange. It may even turn out that this ancient text has something new to teach us about how to redeem sexuality and love in our fallen world.[9]

[9] For an excellent analysis of the relationship of the Song to the story of Creation and the Fall from Eden, see Trible's article and its expanded form in chapter 4 and 5 of *God and the Rhetoric of Sexuality* (Philadelphia: Fortress Press, 1978), pp. 72-165.

FIVE

CONTEXTS, THEMES, AND MOTIFS

WOVEN INTO THE TAPESTRY of the Song are recurrent patterns
of meaning which suggest the presence of literary conventions, in
much the way that Petrarchan themes and imagery are conventional
to Renaissance poetry. To uncover and illuminate recurrent material
in the Song may draw the modern reader closer to its distant cultural
source, while also deepening appreciation of the individual poems and
the collection as a whole. The following discussions are intended to
reveal patterns in the text by illuminating settings and ambiance
(which I call 'contexts'), underlying attitudes and ideas ('themes'), and
repeated images and symbols ('motifs'). These categories were not
fixed in my mind prior to translating; rather their dominance emerged
during and, especially, after the translation process, when I was able to
step back from the text once again and see its shape and contours from
a new vantage point.

Four Basic Contexts
Context as setting is not equally dominant in all the poems of the Song:
some poems depend crucially on setting for their arguments or moods,
while others seem not to 'take place' anywhere in particular, but to
focus more on interior emotional space. But even when the setting of a
poem is not defined, ambiance is usually present to some degree.
Context changes often in the Song, from poem to poem and sometimes
within poems, creating a kaleidoscopic shifting of patterns. Out of this
movement we can isolate four basic contexts which, either separately
or in combination, provide the backdrops for most of the Song's
poems:
  a) the cultivated or habitable countryside;
  b) the wild or remote natural landscape and its elements;
  c) interior environments (houses, halls, rooms);
  d) city streets.

a) All the love dialogues and many of the love monologues take place, at least in part, in the countryside. The pastures of poem 3, the grove of poem 6, the valley and thicket of poem 7, the blossoming spring landscapes of poems 9, 21, and 24, the rocks and ravines of poem 10, the hills of poems 12, 15, and 31, the gardens of poems 18, 19, and 31, and the shade of the quince tree in poem 27 are all tempting and conducive sites for love. Either of the lovers may take the initiative in these settings, which themselves seem to invite lovemaking. The poems which share these lush, idyllic contexts tend to portray young, romantic love: the pleasure of anticipation finds at least as much expression here as the experience of fulfillment. Although the lovers are often separated in the countryside, reunions always seem to be expected there. Thus, in the benign and receptive landscape, invitations to love are playful, suffused with feelings of happy arousal.

The countryside also sets the scene, as background if not foreground, for other types of poems — 2, 11, and 30 — which are not love monologues or dialogues. In each of these, the country is represented by the vineyard, a special kind of place which is discussed as a separate motif. As we have already observed and shall presently see further, the tone of these poems is quite different from that of the ones we have just mentioned.

b) Generally we find nature receptive to lovers in the Song; however there is another kind of natural context in the Song which lends a very different ambiance to several poems. This is the landscape of wild, remote, sometimes dangerous nature: the desert/wilderness of poems 14 and 26, the mountain lairs of wild animals in poem 16, the seas and rivers of poem 28, and the staring eyes of the heavens in poems 2 and 20. These elements of nature suggest distant or overwhelming forces, which can provoke anxiety or a sense of urgency, as in poems 16 and 28, or create a miragelike atmosphere, as in poems 14 and 26, or suggest mystery as in poems 2 and 20. Although these natural elements are sometimes dominant images rather than complete settings, their effect in the poems is always strong; the poems that share this natural ambiance have a different mood from others in the collection, a mood perhaps best characterized as one of awe. In contrast to the countryside setting, intimacy is not supported by this context; here nature can keep the lovers apart or be an awesome backdrop to their union. The expression of love here is not playful but reverent, and sometimes overwhelmed. Not just I-Thou love is expressed in this context, but a variety of emotional experiences, balancing the more predictable range we find in the countryside.

c) Interior environments take several forms in the Song, all of them associated with lovemaking. Thus the king's chambers in poems 1 and 5, the winehall in poem 8, the speaker's bedroom in poems 13 and 19, and the mother's house in poems 13 and 25 are all supportive environments for love. In addition, poem 9 opens with the woman in her house, listening for the voice of her lover, and poem 24 closes with a return from the countryside to the doorways of the lovers' home, where lovemaking will be at its best. The interior environment often encourages the modes of dreams and fantasies, and the imagination seems to have its freest reign here.

Associated twice with the interior context of the home is the mother. (Strikingly, no mention of a father appears in the Song.) The mother's house seems to be the most secure and private environment for love in the Song; for this reason, the speakers of poems 13 and 25 want to take the beloved from the streets and lead him back to the mother's home, where the lovers will be free from public interference. Ironically, the role of the mother is in contrast to the role that brothers sometimes play in other poems: in poems 2 and 29, for example, they seem to want to keep their sister from erotic experience. Brothers, however, need not be hostile figures; in poem 25 the speaker says that *if* her lover *were* her brother, she would feel free to kiss him in the public street, implying that sibling affection (as opposed to lovers' embraces) is both natural and socially acceptable. Public society, as we shall see next, creates a very different context from the microcosm of the home.

d) Of all the contexts of the Song, the city is least sympathetic to the lovers. Thus, the city watchmen are useless to the woman in her search for her lover in poem 13; in poem 19 these guarders of the walls violate the woman. The speaker of poem 25 senses the danger in the public domain: she knows she cannot kiss her beloved in the streets without opening herself to ridicule. The city women (literally, 'daughters of Jerusalem' or 'daughters of Zion') are another group of outsiders whose attitude to the lovers is unsympathetic. In poems 8, 13, and 25 they are adjured not to disturb the lovers; in poem 19, they offer to help the woman find her lost beloved only after they are themselves tempted by the description of his beauty. In poem 2 the city women are the hostile audience for the speech of a woman who seems to live in the countryside, and whose dark beauty is the object of their scorn. (In poem 14, the only other place where these figures appear, they play a different role. They seem to be associated with the court of the king rather than with the urban world, and I have therefore referred to them there as 'Jerusalem's daughters.') Like the city guards, the city women seem to be a foil against which the intimate world-of-two emerges as an ideal, and the poems which have urban settings often express conflict and negative emotions. I explore these ideas further in the ensuing discussions of themes.

* * *

Related to the subject of contexts are proper place names, which appear frequently in the Hebrew text. In Hebrew these names often have great resonance, but in translation they have far less, especially to the modern reader. The places named in the Hebrew include: Jerusalem/Zion, Ein Gedi, Lebanon, Gilead, Amana, Senir, Hermon, Tirza, Heshbon, Bat-Rabbim, Damascus, Carmel, and Baal-Hamon. I retained specific names in the translations whenever I thought they had clear associations for an English reader, or whenever I felt that specificity added, rather than detracted, from the point of the poem. For example, in poem 20, it seemed important to use the names Tirza and Jerusalem rather than to refer to them as 'cities,' because cities in general in the Song provide a different context from the one suggested by the distant vision of them here. However, more often than not, I interpreted the meanings of place names for the English reader, as in the example of 'the slopes' for Mount Gilead, cited in the previous chapter. Other instances of this are given in the discussion of motifs in this chapter, and in the notes to the poems (chapter six); also my discussion of the translation of botanical imagery (under 'motifs') is analogous. I did not strive for consistency in making these choices; as elsewhere, my decisions were based on the demands of the individual poems and what I believed would allow maximum expression in English verse.

Five Themes and Their Variations

The themes I analyze here were isolated for various reasons: to point out conceptual connections among poems, to explain otherwise enigmatic material, and to illuminate the intellectual/emotional fabric from which the poems in the Song were cut. This analysis does not attempt to cover all the thematic material in the Song, but treats instead what plays a dominant or significant, though not necessarily obvious, role. The following five themes not only recur but overlap, representing interwoven threads of meaning in over half the poems of the Song:

a) beckoning the beloved (poems 1, 9, 10, 16, 24, 31);
b) banishment of the beloved — the theme of secret love (poems 12, 15, 31);
c) search for the beloved (poems 3, 13, 19);
d) the self in a hostile world (poems 2, 29, 30);
e) praise of love itself (poems 23, 28).

a) Beckoning the beloved, a classic theme in love poetry of the Western tradition, is central in many of the love monologues and love dialogues in the Song, where both male and female speakers invite the beloved to make love. As might be expected, beckoning is often accompanied by praise; as a part of courting, beckoning is enhanced by the lavishing of compliments. Poems which share this theme portray the idealism and romanticism of courtship and often have a mood of wondrous expectation about them. Their tone tends to be flirtatious and often coy, although sometimes they are also quite passionate.

The literary devices used to beckon the beloved are various. Sometimes praise and entreaties suffice, as in poems 1, 10, and 31. The speakers of poems 9 and 24 describe the lush countryside in an effort to induce the beloved to come away with them. The argument of these poems is that of the classic spring song: all of nature is mating — why not we too? Poem 16, on the other hand, depicts the natural landscape as ominous; the speaker urges his beloved to leave the danger and come away with him.

A linguistic feature associated with the theme of beckoning is the frequent use of verbal imperatives. 'Take me away' (literally, 'pull me') says the speaker of poem 1. In poems 9, 10, 16, and 24, all the speakers use verbal imperatives to extend invitations, which I render consistently with the verb 'come.' I chose this verb in part to suggest thematic similarity among these poems, and partly because more literal translations of these imperatives ('get up,' 'show me,' 'go') sound far too harsh in English, losing the delicate evocativeness of the Hebrew. The first half of poem 31, which also uses an imperative, seemed to me to be so imploring that I rendered the imperative as a request: 'will you let me hear you?'

In part, the pathos of these poems derives from the implied separation of the lovers and their desire to be united. This separation is a part of other themes as well, and is crucial, as we shall see next, to the theme of secret love.

b) In poems 12, 15, and the second half of 31, the male beloved or male speaker is either chased away or voluntarily removes himself from the woman. Poems 12 and 31 may seem particularly puzzling, because the female speaker refers to her beloved with an endearing love name in the same breath that she sends him away. In poem 31, she is responding to her lover's tender invitation; one hardly expects her response to be unfeeling. In fact in neither poem is her tone angry or disinterested, but she is firm in her commands; as in the passages of beckoning, verbal imperatives are used here ('turn round' and 'go' in my translation). What are we to make of this?

The key to these poems lies in viewing the love relationship as a secret affair, which can be consummated only at night, when the lovers are not exposed to scrutiny. By chasing her beloved away in poems 12 and 31, the woman is not rejecting him, only exercising caution. The male speaker acts out of the same motivation at the close of poem 15.

This interpretation is speculative, but it accounts for otherwise enigmatic statements that most standard Bible translations circumvent. For example, the King James and Revised Standard Versions idiosyncratically render *b^erah*, the command spoken by the woman in poem 31, as 'make haste.' The Jerusalem Bible reads 'haste away,' but notes that this is 'an answer by a different author.' The New American Bible apparently determines that the original means exactly the opposite of what it says: its translation reads 'come into the open.' But in Biblical Hebrew *b^erah* is neither rare nor ambiguous: its meaning is not 'come,' or even 'make haste,' but 'flee.' And the Hebrew word *sob* in poem 12 means 'turn,' the implication being 'turn away from me.' Because the Hebrew lines following *sob* in poem 12 (literally, 'make yourself, my beloved, like a gazelle or young stag on the split mountains') are almost identical to those which follow *b^erah* in poem 31 (literally, 'my beloved, make yourself like a gazelle or young stag on the mountains of spices'), there is good reason to associate these passages and to assume that the command in each has similar intent. Furthermore, the Hebrew lines which precede *sob* in poem 12 (literally, 'until the day breathes and the shadows flee') also precede the statement made by the male speaker at the end of poem 15. In the latter, the speaker resolves to go away to the mountains until the day is over. There is, therefore, reason also to link the closing of poem 15 with those of poems 12 and 31. I interpret the difficult phrase 'until the day breathes' as 'until the day is over' for two reasons. First, I assume the shadows are ordinary sun-shadows; thus their departure suggests day's end rather than daybreak. Second, in a hot Mediterranean climate, the day seems to 'breathe' at dusk, when the air begins to cool. In all three poems, the man is expected to remove himself from his beloved by fleeing to the hills, but the phrase 'until the day is over' in poems 12 and 31 limits the extent of the separation. Implied in all three poems is the understanding that the man will return to his beloved later, at night, when they can be safely alone.

Among the poems' contexts, we have seen that the public domain is unsympathetic to the lovers and the city is the setting most threatening to the love relationship. Now we see that sometimes even in the domesticated countryside, where both male and female speakers express the desire to meet, the lovers seem to feel that their rendezvous must be kept secret, confined to nighttime. This may be because of fear of public censure, or it may be a kind of fiction, part of a lovers' game. Whichever it is — reality or game — the theme of secret love explains otherwise baffling statements in at least three poems in the Song, and may deepen our understanding of other poems as well. For example, beckoning may now be seen as an antidote to secrecy: one lover coaxes while the other cautiously hides away. This explains the shyness and coyness of the hidden lover, and the fervor of the one who extends the invitation.

The role of the public, as it relates to the theme of the secret love, has implications for the interpretation of yet other, different kinds of poems. It is especially important in the next two themes.

c) Search for the beloved is the explicit theme of poems 13 and 19. Both poems open in the bedroom and then move into the city streets, where the speaker encounters outsiders. In her searches for her absent beloved, the female speaker first comes upon the city watchmen, who are indifferent to her cause in poem 13 and brutal to her in poem 19. These are the only two poems in which the figures of the guards appear, and it is difficult to speculate about their actual role in the society. However, as representatives of the public — groups of people outside the love relationship — they conform to a general pattern in the Song. They represent the real world, so to speak, against which the ideal world-of-two is contrasted.

Similarly, the city women appear in several poems as disinterested although sometimes hostile spectators, outside the love relationship. When their aid is solicited to find the lost beloved in poem 19, they respond at first skeptically: what's so special about your lover that you make us take an oath? But, after the woman replies with a lengthy and detailed description of him, they are eager to participate in the search. At this point, the speaker turns them away, affirming that she knows where to find her lover after all. The ending of this poem suggests that the searches for the beloved, desperate and frenzied though they seem, may be a literary fiction. That is, the search itself may be a metaphorical way of describing the loss that is felt whenever the beloved is not near, even if the speaker knows exactly where he is. On the other hand, the conclusion of the poem may be the fiction: the woman may be only fantasizing about a reunion with her beloved or bluffing to assert her independence. In either case, when the city women are ready to offer help, they are perceived as intruders. This may also be the reason why in poem 13 they are adjured not to wake or rouse the lovers, that is, not to disturb them in their lovemaking. (For a more detailed explanation of this adjuration, see the note to poem 8 in the next chapter.)

The view of the city searches as metaphors for feelings of loss rather than actual odysseys into the streets sheds light on the pastoral search in poem 3. Here the speaker directly addresses her beloved with the request to know where she can find him when he is pasturing, which is to say, during the day. The question, one deduces, is being asked at night when the lovers are alone. The tone of the whole dialogue is coy rather than frantic, and this makes perfect sense in the context of a lovers' game. It is wrong to find the response of the male speaker cold or harshly evasive. The question itself is asked playfully, and the response implies that the woman is not really in need of an answer: '*If* you don't know,' says the man, implying that she really *does* know where to find him.

While the woman addresses her beloved directly in this poem she also makes reference to outsiders. She does not, she says, want to go about begging the aid of her lover's friends. The friends here play a role similar to that of the city women in other poems. They may not be hostile, but neither can they be expected to be of much help. They too represent the public domain which is repeatedly in conflict with the lovers' desire to be alone together.

d) In poems 2 and 30, which make symbolic reference to erotic experience but are not specifically addressed to the beloved, we see yet another aspect of the role of outsiders in the Song. Both these poems are monologues addressed to figures in the public domain: the city women in one, King Solomon in the other. While neither Solomon nor the city women speak in these poems, we deduce their attitudes from the defiant and even indignant tone of the monologues.

The purpose of the posture struck by the speakers of poems 2 and 30 is self-assertion. In both poems the speakers present themselves in contrast to the outside world. Thus in poem 2 the speaker asserts that she is black *and* beautiful despite the fact that others, the city women, may consider her dark skin unattractive. In poem 30 the speaker argues that his vineyard, a symbol for his beloved, is more valuable to him than the king's. In both poems, the love relationship provides the speakers with courage to confront the public world.

Similarly, the female speaker in the dialogue poem 29 rejects the protectiveness of her brothers by first asserting her attractiveness and independence and then stating that her self-worth has been confirmed by her lover. Like the brothers in poem 2, the men in this poem seem to have a punitive attitude toward their younger sister, who responds to them with a proud defiance of their authority.

Indignation, defiance, fear, and hostility are emotions that all have their parts in the Song, emerging often, as we have seen, in connection with the public domain. We find in the Song that love of self, like love of another, often meets opposition from the outside world, but is supported by the smaller world-of-two.

e) Explicit in only two poems but implied in almost all the poems in the collection is praise of love itself. As the opening lines of poem 23 exclaim: 'Of all pleasure, how sweet / Is the taste of love!' While poem 23 does not continue in this vein, but shifts to praise of the beloved, poem 28 is devoted almost entirely to praise of love. In this sense, poem 28 is unique in the collection, and distinguishes itself further by its hyperbole and powerful imagery. It is the only poem in the Song which mentions death, pitting death against love in a contest for power. Love does not conquer death, but neither is it conquered by it. Love blazes despite all attempts to extinguish it.

The opening lines of poem 23 and the middle stanzas of poem 28 make two different statements about love: while the one proclaims the joy of love, the other asserts its power. Taken together, these two appreciations represent the polarities that lend texture to the tapestry of the whole text. The themes treated above indicate that the emotional fabric of the Song is not wholly joyful, but sometimes interwoven with tensions and struggle. These aspects of particular love relationships are shown to be the nature of love itself in poems 23 and 28. Taken as a whole, the Song expresses the paradoxes of love in the world: conflict which intensifies passion, painful separation which heightens the pleasure of union, bonding which gives the individual courage to stand alone.

Six Central Motifs

Interwoven among the dominant themes of the Song are other, lighter strands of meaning: images and symbols embroidered into the design of the tapestry. These are what I call motifs; the following recur most often and seem most prominent:

  a) flora and fauna, and artifice, as complementary sources of imagery;
  b) the vines and the vineyard, as a special place and as metaphors and symbols;
  c) the garden, as a special place and as an extended metaphor;
  d) eating and drinking as erotic metaphors;
  e) regality and wealth, as metaphors, figures, and foils;
  f) sensuality and the senses.

  a) The references to flora and fauna in the Song are so many and so various that the Song has come to be thought of as nature poetry. It is true that ' "nature poetry" is a clumsy term,' as the poet Wendell Berry points out, 'for there is a sense in which most poetry is nature poetry; most poets, even those least interested in nature, have found in the world an abundant stock of symbols and metaphors.'[1] But in the Song, flora and fauna are fundamental: they abound everywhere, in foregrounds and backgrounds, as real, metaphorical, and symbolic. Plants and animals appear as depictions of the natural landscape (as in poems 3, 6, 9, 16, 19, 21, 24, 27, and 31), as metaphors for the beloved (for example, in poems 4, 5, 7, 9, 10, 12, 18, 23, and 31), and as metaphors for parts of the human body (the best examples of these are in the *wasfs*). The animals in the Song include the mare, dove, gazelle, deer, nightingale ('songbird' in my translation), turtledove ('dove' in my translation), fox, lion, leopard, and raven. Most of these are identifiable by their Hebrew common names, although the standard English Bibles give somewhat differing translations for a few: for example, 'stag' or 'hart' for deer, 'jackal' for fox. The plants mentioned in the Song are even more numerous — over twenty-five varieties of trees, shrubs, flowers, herbs, fruits, nuts, spices, and nectars — and

---

[1] 'A Secular Pilgrimage,' *The Hudson Review*, 23 (1970), 401.

their identification is more problematic. Because botanical images are
so numerous and so recurrent in the Song, I will comment on their
identification, interpretation, and translation before discussing their
relationship to the world of artifice.

Like most botanical references in the Bible, those in the Song are
difficult to identify because their common names do not necessarily
correspond to modern Hebrew usage. For example, while today the
word *tappuaḥ* means apple, it must have meant something else in the
Bible, because apples were not indigenous to ancient Israel. The
translations in standard English Bibles and other versions of the Song
tend to be misleading because the translators have hardly investigated
the original referents of Biblical plant names.[2] While some modern
versions depart from the traditional translations, they often do no
more than guess about the meanings of these words, and they rarely go
so far as to attempt to determine the impact that plant images might
have had in their original poetic contexts. The faithful translation of
botanical imagery in the Song requires three stages: first, accurate
identification of the referent of the Biblical Hebrew plant name;
second, interpretation of the meaning and resonance of the image in its
poetic context; third, choice of the English word or phrase that will
both evoke the original landscape and be consonant with the tone of
the new English poem.

I was greatly assisted in the first stage by Neot Kedumim: The
Gardens of Israel. The staff of Neot Kedumim have done important
research in the field of Biblical botany; by consulting native speakers
of languages which are cognate with Hebrew but which, unlike
Hebrew, have retained the same common botanical names over the
centuries, they have identified many of the plants named in the Bible.
In addition, by studying the modern Israeli landscape, they have been
able to make reasonable conjectures about its vegetation in Biblical
times. I considered the information provided by Neot Kedumim to be
authoritative in most cases, and I used it as the basis for the next two
stages, the interpretation of meaning and the choice of English
equivalents.

I have indicated my approach to interpretation and translation in
previous chapters; essentially the same principles and methods apply
to my translations of botanical imagery. For example, when a flower
was used as a metaphor, I tried first to determine whether the point of

[2] An exception is the work of G. R. Driver in the translation of *The New
English Bible*.

the comparison was visual beauty or texture or fragrance. I then searched for an equivalent image in English, one that would have similar impact on the modern reader. I tried, as often as possible, to name in English the same plants named in the Hebrew, but if these plants had particularly inappropriate associations today (as in the case of myrrh and frankincense, discussed in the note to poem 14, in the next chapter), or if the English names were awkward or archaic, I found alternate expressions. Sometimes I substituted descriptions for specific names (such as 'sweet fruit tree growing wild' for *tappuaḥ;* see the note to poem 7) and sometimes I named plants of closely related species. I did not translate botanical images consistently from poem to poem, but let the various demands of the individual poems guide my decisions. For example, I translated the *šošannah* (narcissus) at different moments as 'narcissus,' 'lily,' 'daffodil,' 'wildflower,' and sometimes simply 'flower'; in some cases, I used different translations within a single poem, in order to stress a particular point in English (see, for example, poem 7 and the note to it in the next chapter). Although I translated these images with considerable flexibility, I tried throughout to respect the integrity of the original landscape by never naming plants that could not have been part of it; I also did not name plants that would be unfamiliar or meaningless to modern English readers.

The decisions made in translating botanical images were difficult because these images, more than most others, convey specific, culture-bound information that resists transmigration. Plants tend not to be hardy travelers, so one must make a special effort to keep them alive through the journey in order finally to transplant them without endangering their vitality.

Although plant and animal imagery is found throughout the Song, it is by no means the exclusive source of metaphor. Even in the *waṣfs*, which rely heavily on natural imagery, metaphors are borrowed from the realms of artifice — art, craft, and architecture — and these seem to mingle freely with metaphors from nature. Thus in the *waṣf* of poem 19, the man's hair is black as a raven, his eyes are like doves, his cheeks like spices, his lips like flowers, and his stature or appearance like cedars in the mountains; but his arms are cylinders of gold studded with jewels, his belly is a slab of ivory inlaid with gems, and his legs are marble columns set on gold stands — all images of sculptural and architectural forms. His overall appearance is described at the outset as bright and red, suggesting the brilliance of gold and jewels, but toward the end his palate is described as 'sweet,' a word elsewhere applied to fruit. Similarly, in the *wasf* of poem 15, the woman's lips are like threads of silk and her neck like a tower adorned with shields, images of artifice and architecture interspersed among other images from nature: doves, goats, sheep, pomegranates, fawns. So too in the *wasf* of poem 22, where the thighs like spinning jewels are the artisan's handicraft, the towerlike neck and face suggest architectural grandeur, but the natural landscape — of wheat, flowers, pools, and mountains — lends images for other parts of the body.[3]

In addition to the imagery of the artisans, the world of military society provides images for certain poems in the Song. The tower in poem 15 is hung with the shields of warriors; the wall, door, and turrets of poem 29 suggest the structure of a fortress; in poem 14, sixty sword-bearing warriors attend the procession of the king.

The argument of poem 4 makes explicit what is implied throughout the Song: while the beloved is naturally beautiful, the speaker sees no harm in gilding the lily. In the world of the Song, artifice does not compete with nature, but complements it. Similar to other contrasts we have observed — such as those between public and private domains or separation and union of lovers — the relationship between the natural world and the world of human artifacts is mutually intensifying, and contributes to the density of the Song's texture.

b) The words *kerem*, 'vineyard,' and *gepen*, 'vine,' appear in eight poems in the Song, often more than once in each. I have translated these words in various ways — 'vine,' 'vineyard,' 'grapevine,' 'grapes' — depending upon the needs of English verse. For the sake of this discussion, however, I will revert to a stricter distinction between the two Hebrew words.

Kerem appears in poems 2, 5, 11, 24, and 30; *gepen* in poems 9, 21, 23, and 24. In poems 9, 21 and 24, *gepen* refers to the grapevine in the

---

[3] Because the imagery of artifice in the *wasfs* is so vivid, it is perhaps not surprising that scholars have speculated about its parallels to visual forms in ancient art. For example, Gillis Gerleman, in 'Die Bildsprache des Hohen-liedes und die altägyptische Kunst,' *Annual of the Swedish Theological Institute*, 1 (1962), 24–30, has proposed that many of the images in the *wasfs* are based on figures from ancient Egyptian sculpture and bas relief. Although there may be some valid parallels here, Gerleman's theory is far too limiting. By viewing the *wasfs* as descriptions of statues rather than as metaphorical portrayals of the human body, he misses the relationship between nature and artifice at the core of this poetry.

stage of budding or early fruit, when it gives forth fragrance. All three of these poems are spring songs, and the *gepen* is one of the details in the springtime landscape. In all three, the budding vines are also associated with erotic experience, invited or anticipated by one of the lovers. In poem 23, *gepen* appears in the phrase *eškᵉlot haggepen*, 'clusters of the vine'; here the reference is to the mature fruit, and I have rendered it 'clusters of grapes.' The point of the reference is also different: here *gepen* is a metaphor for the woman's breasts; thus it is appropriate that the ripe fruit is evoked, rather than the flower.

The word *kerem* is also used in various ways in the poems. In poem 24 it is straightforward: like the fields where the henna blooms, it is an appealing, outdoor site where the lovers meet. In poem 5 it also describes a place, but not specifically a vineyard; it is attached to the proper name Ein Gedi, where the poem says, *koper*, 'henna' ('blossoms' in my translation), is found. Because Ein Gedi is an oasis and henna does not grow on vines, the *kerem* of poem 5 seems not to be a vineyard but a general place of vegetation, and I have rendered it here as 'oasis.'

The references to *kerem* in poems 5 and 24 suggest that the word has somewhat different meanings in different poems, although in both instances it refers to a place of vegetation. Poems 2, 11, and 30 suggest an even wider range of meanings for *kerem*, because it is impossible to interpret these poems coherently without symbolism. In each of these poems, *kerem* is mentioned several times, and once in each it is in the first person possessive construct: 'my vineyard' in poems 2 and 30, 'our vineyards' in poem 11. In poems 2 and 30 an emphatic modifier follows the construct form — *karmi šelli*, 'my vineyard which is mine' — which I have translated in both instances as 'my own.' The female speaker of poem 2 says that she has been made to watch the vineyards and has not watched her own; the male speaker of poem 30 says that Solomon has a prosperous vineyard but that his, the speaker's, own vineyard is more precious to him than Solomon's. Both poems suggest that the vineyard is more than a place; it seems also to be a symbol for female sexuality. When the woman speaks of her vineyard, she refers to herself; when the man speaks of his vineyard, he refers to his beloved. In poem 2, the woman alludes to not having guarded her own sexuality, implying that she has had erotic experience. In poem 30, the speaker asserts that his beloved is all his own, not to be shared with anyone else.

Poem 11 contains the most cryptic of all the references to *kerem*, because it is unclear in this poem who is speaking and to whom. But once again the poem makes most sense if we understand the *kerem* symbolically: the foxes (a masculine noun in the Hebrew) are raiding the vineyards and therefore must be caught; the vineyards seem to be symbols for women.

It should not seem problematic to find *kerem* used in several different ways in the collection; the different meanings enhance each other's resonances, while the internal coherence of the individual poems remains intact.

c) The garden, like the vineyard, appears in several different poems in the Song, sometimes as a location and sometimes as a metaphor for the female beloved. Even when it refers to a location, however, it is generally associated with the woman, and it sometimes simultaneously symbolizes her.

In poem 31, the garden is the place where the female beloved is situated; in the penultimate stanza of poem 19, it is a place entered by a male. The Hebrew verb *yarad* (literally, 'went down,' rendered 'has gone to walk' in my translation) which precedes the word *ganno*, 'his garden,' in the penultimate stanza of 19 is the same as the verb in poem 21 (where I translate it 'walking'). The walnut orchard of poem 21 is literally a 'walnut garden,' to which the speaker 'goes down' to observe the opening of the flowers. In poem 19, the male 'goes down' to 'his garden' to pasture and gather flowers. The links between these two passages — the same verb in both and the reference to flowers or flowering — make a strong argument for viewing the otherwise unidentifiable speaker of poem 21 as male. The association of the garden with the female beloved in poem 31 further suggests a symbolic level of meaning in both poems 19 and 21: the garden represents the female beloved, who is entered ('gone down to') by the male; the gathering and eating of flowers are other male sexual activities, and the opening of the flowers may be an allusion to female sexuality.

In poem 18, the garden is explicitly erotic. Whereas in poems 19, 21, and 31 the garden *can* be viewed simply as a place and not a symbol, in poem 18, it functions as an extended metaphor describing the beloved. The word *gan*, 'garden,' appears five times in this Hebrew poem, three times in the possessive construct ('my garden' and 'his garden'). Like the vineyard in poems 2 and 30, the garden in poem 18 can be 'owned' by either the woman or the man, but it seems to refer in both cases to female sexuality. Thus the woman calls upon the winds to breathe upon *ganni*, 'my garden,' wishing that her beloved will come to *ganno*, 'his garden.' These two references are, of course, to the same garden, and to avoid awkwardness and confusion in the English, I omitted the phrase 'his garden' entirely. The point is made clear in the following stanza, in which the male speaker replies to his beloved, 'I have come to my garden.'

As in poem 19, the male speaker in poem 18 gathers plants (here spices rather than flowers) in his garden, and also feasts there. Because poem 18 is controlled by an extended metaphor in which the female is compared to the garden itself, to the water that flows in it, and to all the vegetation (fruits, flowers, woods, spices) that grows in it, the activities of the male in the garden — entering, gathering, and eating — must be seen as erotic. The use of the garden as an extended metaphor in poem 18 (analyzed in more detail in the note to this poem, in the next chapter) suggests ways to view the motif of eating and drinking in other poems as well.

d) The Hebrew root *'kl*, 'eat,' appears three times in the Song, all in poem 19. In all three cases I have avoided the English word 'eat' because of its somewhat vulgar tone; I have used instead the words 'share,' 'taste,' and 'feast.' The female speaker in the poem expresses the wish that her beloved will come to his garden and eat its choice fruits; the male speaker replies that he has come, he has gathered spices, he has eaten his honey and drunk his wine and milk. At the conclusion of the poem, a third voice enjoins the two lovers to eat and drink, even to intoxication ('drink deeply' in my translation). Clearly, eating and drinking are symbols for erotic experience; the association of eating and drinking with the garden, and with the activity of gathering in particular, suggests that erotic overtones may be implied also in other contexts where there is allusion to eating and drinking.

For example, in the penultimate stanza of poem 19, the woman says that her beloved has gone down to his garden *lir'ot*, 'to pasture' (translated in my version 'to feed his sheep'), and to gather flowers. In the last stanza she calls him *haro'eh bassosannim*, 'the one who pastures among the flowers,' an appellation that appears in poem 12 as well (I translate it, in both instances, 'Who leads his flock to feed / Among the flowers'). The Hebrew word for pasturing, or feeding one's flocks, also appears in poem 3: the female speaker there asks her beloved where he pastures ('where you feed your sheep' in my version); and the male speaker replies by telling her to pasture her own flocks among the fields of the other 'ones who pasture' ('the shepherds' in my translation). In all these cases where *r'h* appears, whether as a noun or as a verb, there is an implied second level of meaning. Because pasturing is associated with the garden, with flowers, and with gathering — all of which have erotic associations, especially when they appear together — there is the suggestion that pasturing means not only feeding one's flock but feeding oneself, that is, participating in sexual activity. Because the garden and its flowers are associated with female sexuality, pasturing is usually symbolic of male sexual activity. The one who pastures in the flowers is always a male; the only suggestion that a woman ever pastures at all is in poem 3, where no flowers are mentioned.

There are other, more direct references to eating and drinking in the Song, and these too have erotic associations. In poem 7, the female speaker says that her beloved's fruit is sweet to her palate (rendered 'I taste your love' in my translation); here the male is compared to a fruit tree, and the female speaker finds pleasure in dwelling in his shadow and tasting his fruit. In poem 8, the female speaker asks to be refreshed and sustained with raisincakes and quinces — an unusual request for one who is 'sick with love.' It seems that the real nourishment she seeks is not food but her lover's attention, about which she fantasizes in the succeeding lines.

The food most emphatically associated with lovemaking in the Song is wine. More than once it is mentioned by way of complimenting the beloved — for example, that her mouth is like good wine (poem 23), or that her lovemaking is better than wine (poem 17), or that *his* lovemaking is better than wine (poem 1). The speaker of poem 17 goes on to praise his beloved in detail, not failing to mention the taste of honey and milk on her tongue, and thus making explicit the association between lovemaking and food. Honey and milk (probably a 'fixed pair,' a convention of oral poetry) are linked with wine in poem 18 as well. In both poems, honey and milk lend added sweetness to the wine imagery, and reinforce the erotic suggestions.

The image of wine is perhaps nowhere more erotic than in poem 25, where it is in parallel position to the nectar of pomegranates. The speaker of this poem offers to take her beloved to her mother's home, where she will give him spiced wine and the juice of her pomegranate to drink. The pomegranate, long recognized as a fertility symbol in ancient culture, is mentioned in connection with the woman several times in the Song — as a fruit of the gardens in poems 18 and 21, and as a metaphor for her forehead in the *wasfs*. In poem 25 it seems to be a symbol, like the vineyard, for the woman's sexuality: the first person possessive construct, 'my pomegranate,' emphasizes this. The lines that follow this image are the same as those that follow the request for food in poem 8 (which, incidentally, takes place in a winehall); both allusions to feasting lead the woman to fantasize about her beloved's embrace. Feasting, it seems, almost always has erotic overtones in the Song, and wine is the most intoxicating temptation to the feast.

e) Like the other motifs treated here, the motif of regality is used in a variety of ways in the Song, but, unlike the others, its connotations can be either positive or negative. For example, when the beloved is compared to a king, as in poems 1 and 5, the regal image is clearly a compliment, a way of expressing affection and esteem. This is also the effect of calling the woman a princess in poem 22, and of stating that she captures kings — as if to say she could attract anyone. In poem 2, the regal image of King Solomon's tapestries also has positive associations — it is a metaphor for the speaker's dark and lovely skin.

But in other poems, regality acts as a foil for the speaker or the beloved. The most vehement assertion is in poem 30, in which the speaker contrasts his own vineyard with the king's, and judges his own to be superior. Similarly, but without defiance, the speaker of poem 20 sets his beloved against a backdrop of sixty queens, and proclaims her so evidently special that even they sing her praises. In both poems, the speaker contrasts the uniqueness of his beloved with the multitude of the regal holdings. The vineyard in poem 30 brings in a fortune (the Hebrew specifies one thousand pieces of silver); in poem 20, the queens, concubines ('brides' in my translation), and young women, who are all the possessions of the king, number in the scores. But these large numbers, signifying affluence and luxury, cannot compete, in the speaker's eyes, with his one, own beloved. He would not, he declares in poem 30, trade his beloved for all of King Solomon's harem.

Wealth cannot compete with love, suggest the speakers of these poems. The female speaker of poem 28 asserts even more emphatically that a man is to be scorned if he attempts to buy love in the marketplace. Even were he to offer, as the Hebrew indicates, 'all the wealth of his house,' he could never purchase love with his money.

Wealth, however, like regality, has more than one connotation in the Song. In poem 4 the speaker offers to adorn his beloved with gold and silver, and here the offer is *not* met with scorn: gold and silver are fitting gifts because they are offered in the spirit of love. In poem 14, the poem in which regality is most dominant, the splendors of wealth — gold, silver, and cedar adornments — are appropriate to the king's wedding procession. The exquisite appeal of the imagery in this poem

— the smells of the incense, the colors of the carriage — makes regality and wealth seem enthralling; as fervently as they are elsewhere challenged, they are celebrated here. This attests once again to the benefit of viewing the poems in the Song as discrete units, for those who hold that the Song is a unity have to deny the king his due in poems like this, where he is clearly the subject of admiration.

f) By now it should be apparent that the Song is a text extraordinarily rich with sensory imagery. By far the most prevalent sensory material in the text is visual (especially in the *wasfs*); in addition, the sense of sight and references to visions are recurrent motifs in several places (in poem 20; also in poem 17, where a flash of the beloved's eyes thrills the heart). The olfactory sense is also extremely dominant; witness the many references to flowers, fruits, spices, perfumes, and even the aroma of the Lebanon mountains. The sense of taste is evoked in several poems, always seeming to suggest erotic experience. Sound is used less metaphorically, but the sounds of voices are important erotic enticements (as in poems 9, 10, 19, and 31); and, of course, sound plays are abundant in the construction of the Hebrew verse itself, alliteration being a favorite poetic device. The sense of touch is evoked with every wish for the lover's embrace (for example, in the couplets preceding the adjuration in poems 8 and 25) and is further implied in some of the more elusive metaphors, 'breasts like fawns' in poems 15 and 22, and breasts like 'clusters of grapes' in poem 23). Finally, synesthesia, the association of an image perceived by one of the senses with an image perceived by another, is used for poetic effect in the association of a name, as evoked or heard, with a sweet fragrance (poem 1).

While I have not treated each of the senses as a separate motif, their importance is, I hope, apparent from the discussions of the other motifs to which they relate. Indeed, there is probably nothing more essential to appreciation of poetic effect in the Song than a readiness to respond to sensuality.

SIX

NOTES TO THE POEMS

THE NOTES which follow treat selected matters of interpretation in the individual poems; much of what is discussed is based on the preceding chapters. Whenever lines of the Hebrew or English poems are cited by number, they refer to the lines of the poems as presented above in my reconstruction of the text and translation. For example, poem 1, line 1 of the English is: 'O for your kiss! For your love.' When chapter and verse are cited, however, they refer to the traditional divisions which appear in Hebrew and English Bibles. Although the Hebrew and English poems correspond by number, the line numbers of each do not always correspond. For example, the first line in the Hebrew poem 12 is equivalent to the first two lines of the English translation. Whenever possible, I direct my comments to the English poems, but often I need to refer to the Hebrew to make a point. For readers who do not know Hebrew, word-for-word translations are provided when the Hebrew is cited and its meaning is not apparent from the context. When alternate readings of the word or phrase are given, they are set off by commas and the word 'OR' in capitals. Thus in the literal translation, 'Your name is poured, OR green, oil,' 'green' is an alternate reading for 'poured.' The abbreviations used in this chapter (for the Hebrew edition of the Masoretic text, the most frequently consulted lexicon, and the most frequently cited versions and commentaries) are listed at the back of the book.

Title
Chapter 1, verse 1 of the Hebrew is the title of the work and not part of any poem. Literally, the title is 'the song of songs which is by, OR to, OR of, OR about, Solomon.' 'The song of songs' is a superlative construction like 'king of kings' or 'holy of holies,' and probably means 'the greatest of all songs.' Another possible reading is 'the song composed of songs,'

referring to its being a compilation of shorter poems. The word *ʾaˇšer,* 'which,' appears nowhere else in the text; instead the prefix *še-* is used thirty-two times; this is evidence that the title is an editorial addition. The preposition preceding Solomon's name can have any of several meanings. It is not clear whether those who composed the title were attributing authorship of the Song to Solomon, or were dedicating the Song to him, or were claiming it to have been part of the royal possessions. The same preposition occurs with David's name in the opening lines of the Psalms, where it probably was meant to indicate that the Psalms 'belonged to' King David's collection, that is, were written by him. While for centuries tradition viewed the Song as Solomon's creation, today few if any scholars believe that Solomon had anything to do with the composition of the text.

Contrary to popular misconceptions, Solomon is neither a speaker nor a principal character in the Song. His name appears elsewhere in the Hebrew in six instances (poem 2, poem 14 three times, poem 30 twice), where I have sometimes rendered 'the king.' In none of these poems is he the speaker, and only in poem 14 is he the primary focus of attention. As I explain in chapter five, the references to Solomon and to 'the king' seem to be part of a literary motif, used to create poetic contrasts. It is unlikely that the historical person King Solomon is a persona in any of the poems.

The Hebrew title is notable for its delightful alliterations: *šir haˇšširim ʾaˇšer liˇšlomoh.* In English, the book goes by several names — 'The Song of Songs,' 'The Song of Solomon,' 'Canticles' — but 'The Song of Songs,' commonly abbreviated 'the Song,' is the title most used by scholars today.

Poem 1

The opening two lines of the Hebrew have a confusing grammatical feature: the pronominal suffixes shift from third to second person. Similarly, in lines 6 and 7 of the Hebrew, the reference shifts from second person back to third. Thus, KJV translates lines 1-2, 'Let him kiss me with the kisses of his mouth: for thy love is better than wine,' and lines 6-7, 'Draw me, we will run after thee: the King hath brought me into his chambers.' But this translation, which implies a shift of reference from one character to another, is misleading. In fact, the change of person is characteristic of Biblical style and should not be understood as a change of referent. (So agree most commentators. See, for example, Theophile J. Meek, IB, p.103, or Robert Gordis, *The Song of Songs* [New York: Jewish Theological Seminary, 1961], p.78.) The assumption of a third character here would violate the lyric I-Thou relationship in the poem, and make the causal relationship in the syntax — 'Let *him* kiss me . . . *for thy* love is better than wine' — peculiar. It is better to understand the addressed beloved and the third person as the same figure. As in poem 5, 'the king' should be read as a metaphor for the beloved. To emphasize this I have introduced a simile into line 6 of the English: 'Like a king to his rooms —.'

Note too that the verb in the first line of the Hebrew, *yiššaqeni*, is translated by KJV and most others as a jussive: '*let* him kiss me.' The imperfect aspect in Hebrew (Biblical Hebrew does not have verbal tenses as such, but two aspects, perfect and imperfect) can sometimes have this jussive sense of wish or command. In this poem it expresses the mode of wishing found often in love monologues spoken by women in the Song. I rendered the jussive here as 'O for your kiss!'

The Hebrew line 4 reads, literally, 'Your name is poured, OR green, oil.' Oil, throughout the Song, refers to fragrant oils used as perfumes; hence the point is that the name is sweet-smelling. Because of its inappropriate associations in English, I have not used the word 'oil' in the translations.

In what sense, we may ask, can a name be fragrant? The reference may be to the utterance of the name as part of erotic activity, as suggested in the NAB translation: 'Your name spoken is a spreading perfume —.' Perhaps too, the name evokes pleasant memories, as fragrances can. The synesthetic image of a sweet name is emphasized in the Hebrew by a semantic alliteration, *šemen turaq šᵉmeka*.[1]

[1] For another powerful poetic association of a name with the sense of smell, consider these lines from Middle Kingdom Egyptian verse (ca. 2000-1630 B.C.E.):

Behold, my name is detested,
Behold, more than the smell of vultures
On a summer's day when the sky is hot.

Behold, my name is detested,
Behold, [more than the smell of] a catch of fish
On a day of catching when the sky is hot.

Behold, my name is detested,
Behold, more than the smell of ducks,
More than a covert of reeds full of waterfowl.

Behold, my name is detested,
Behold, more than the smell of fishermen,
More than the creeks of the marshes where they have fished.   *[cont.]*

Poem 2

This is one of the most controversial poems in the text. Spoken by a woman to an audience of hostile outsiders, the city women, literally, 'the daughters of Jerusalem,' it is a statement of self-affirmation and pride. Most commentators, however, read the poem, in particular the opening line, as an apology; and most translations reflect this interpretation. Virtually all standard English renditions translate the conjunction in line 1 as 'but,' as in KJV: 'I am swarthy but comely.' But the Hebrew conjunction w^{e^-} means 'and' as well as 'but'; the standard translations are based on the unfortunate assumption that blackness and loveliness are necessarily contradictory.

I believe that the woman's assertion of her blackness is affirmative, not apologetic, and that the tension in the poem is the result of conflict between her and her audience. While the city women stare at her with critical eyes, the speaker defies them to diminish her own self-esteem. No, she argues, I will not be judged by your standards; I am black *and* I am beautiful. Thus, the images in the first stanza are in synonymous parallelism: the tents of the nomadic tribe of Kedar and the drapes of King Solomon are each dark and attractive veils. There is a bit of mystery in these images; the speaker asserts that the stares of others will not penetrate the outer cloak of her skin.

She knows that she is the object of hostile observation, but she is used to such attention. The sun itself has gazed at her, burning her black with its stare, but also, perhaps, admiring her. The poem resounds with underlying paradoxes: light which causes blackness and light which is contained in blackness. These ideas are buried in the roots of central words. The root *šzp* means 'burn,' but it also means 'glance': the eye of the heavens glances and, glancing, burns. It burns the woman 'black,' *šeḥorah*, and again 'black-black,' *šeḥarḥoret*. The root of these words, *šḥr*, is the same as the root of *šaḥar*, meaning 'dawn' or, originally, 'the light before the dawn.' The woman is radiant in her blackness, glowing as the source of light that burned her. Hence,

[cont.]

> Behold, my name is detested,
> Behold, more than the smell of crocodiles,
> More than sitting by ⌈sandbanks⌉ full of crocodiles.

The smell here, of course, is unpleasant rather than sweet; this poem is not erotic. From 'The Man Who Was Tired of Life,' trans. R. O. Faulkner in William Kelly Simpson, ed., *The Literature of Ancient Egypt* (New Haven and London: Yale Univ. Press, 1973), p. 205. The brackets in line 5 indicate erroneous omission; the half brackets in line 15 mean the word is uncertain.

'Black as the light before the dawn,' in line 8 of my translation.

The last stanza presents the greatest difficulties and ambiguities in the poem. It is unclear why the brothers are angry with the speaker, and whether her assignment as keeper of vineyards is a punishment meted out to her because she has neglected herself or whether the self-neglect is a result of the difficult task they assign her. In either case the vineyards, discussed in the previous chapter, are here a sexual symbol: 'my own' vineyard refers to the speaker's self; the statement that she has neglected her own vines is an allusion to having had sexual experience. Implied is the violation of a moral norm, but it is difficult to say exactly what this norm is. I did not try to resolve these problems of interpretation in my translation, but chose instead to let the ambiguities stand as they do in the Hebrew.

Poem 3

The meaning of k^e 'oṭyah in line 4 of the Hebrew, which I translate 'go searching blindly,' is uncertain. KJV translates 'as one that turneth aside'; RSV gives 'like one who wanders.' KB (p. 695) suggests 'wrapped, covered,' and Meek reads 'as one who is veiled,' arguing that the veil is that of a temple prostitute (IB, p. 107). Meek points out that RSV's reading is based on the emendation of the word to k^eṭo 'iyyah, following the Syriac, Symmachus, and Vulgate versions. RSV's reading makes sense in context, but so do the meanings 'covered' or 'veiled,' if we understand by them that the woman is unable to see clearly and find her way to her lover. My translation 'go searching blindly' incorporates these various ideas and is intended to emphasize the hide-and-seek theme of the poem.

Poem 4

The opening lines of the Hebrew read, literally, 'To a mare in Pharaoh's chariotry I compare you, my beloved.' This image is puzzling when one realizes that only stallions, never mares, drew chariots in ancient Egypt. The meaning of the lines only becomes clear when we understand the function of mares in ancient warfare; a passage from Egyptian literature suggests that they were set loose in battle by the enemy to allure and distract the Pharaoh's stallions. Thus the point of the image is not simply that the beloved is as beautiful as a regal horse, as most translations suggest, but that she is as tempting, as distracting, as dangerous even, as the presence of a single mare among many stallions.[2] Believing that this metaphor would have been clear to the original audience, I chose to make it explicit in English: 'Like a mare among stallions.' I omitted mention of Pharaoh because it would have obfuscated rather than illuminated the point.

In the third and fourth lines, the words *torim* and *ḥaruzim* are difficult. The former has uncertain meaning in context; the latter occurs only once in the Bible (a *hapax legomenon*). Most translations give 'ornaments' or the like for *torim*; NJPS translates, 'plaited wreaths.' I go a step further and read plaited hair ('braids' in line 3 of the English). For *ḥaruzim*, usually taken to mean some kind of beads, I read (with KB, p. 332) 'string of shells' ('shells' in line 4 of the English). Thus the woman is described as adorned, but with natural rather than artificial ornaments. The description of the cheeks and necks is appropriate to the original metaphor, for the Egyptians decorated the heads and necks of their horses. It also contrasts nicely with the images of the closing couplet in which the speaker offers his beloved more elaborate ornamentation: braids not of hair but of gold, studded with *nequddot*, 'points, OR bells' of silver. The act of adorning the beloved with gifts establishes the speaker's place in the love relationship.

Thus, the poem moves from a distant view of the beloved to an

---

[2] The following passage is from 'The Biography of Amen-em-heb,' trans. John A. Wilson, in James B. Pritchard, ed., *Ancient Near Eastern Texts Relating to the Old Testament* (Princeton: Princeton Univ. Press, 1955), p. 241: 'Then, when the Prince of Kadesh sent out a mare, which *[was swift]* on her feet and which entered among the army, I ran after her on foot, carrying my *dagger*, and I (ripped) open her belly. I cut off her tail and set it before the king. Praise was given to god for it.' At the word 'army,' the translator notes, 'To stampede the stallions of the Egyptian chariotry.' This seems to testify to the use of mares as strategic ploys in ancient warfare, the implication being that they were successful at distracting the chariot-harnessed stallions of the enemy. After coming to this conclusion, I was happy to find my interpretation substantiated by Marvin H. Pope in his article, 'A Mare in Pharaoh's Chariotry,' *Bulletin of the American Schools of Oriental Research*, No. 200 (December, 1970), pp. 56-61. Pope states (pp. 59 and 61), 'Pharaoh's chariots, like other chariotry in antiquity, were not drawn by a mare or mares but by stallions hitched in pairs. . . . the point of the comparison of the Lady Love with a mare in Pharaoh's chariotry in the Song of Songs 1:9 is that she is the ultimate in sex appeal.' Pope's article provides extensive documentation for this argument. The argument also appears in Pope's commentary, *The Song of Songs* (New York: Doubleday, 1977), pp. 336-341. It is interesting, too, that Rabbinic commentators in the *Midrash Rabbah* and *The Sayings of the Fathers According to Rabbi Nathan* may have read these lines similarly, as Pope also notes.

intimate portrait of her cheeks and neck, and finally concludes with the affirmation of the I-Thou relationship. It is a highly compressed and tightly structured lyric which achieves significant movement in very few lines.

Poem 5

The problematic word in this poem is *bimsibbo* in the first line, which KJV translates, 'at his table,' and RSV translates, 'on his couch.' The Septuagint reads *anaklesis*, 'leaning back, OR reclining,' and it may be from this that RSV derives its meaning. 'Reclining' suggests the more private context of the bedroom with its couch for love, rather than the dining hall, so RSV's reading may be appropriate. However, I take *bimsibbo* to mean something like 'in his surroundings,' from the root *sbb*, 'go around.' The first line thus means, 'Until the king is back in his surroundings,' and I render 'Until the king returns.' My intention was to focus in the opening line on the feelings of anticipation which suffuse the poem as a whole.

The specific fragrance mentioned in the Hebrew is nard, but it may be an allusion to sexual odor. There is no need to interpret the opening prepositional phrase, *'ad-še-*, as referring to spatial distance. The more likely meaning 'until' suggests that the woman exudes aromas in anticipation of her lover's return.

Poem 6

At the suggestion of Chaim Rabin (in personal conversation and correspondence, August-September, 1972), I read the phrase *'enayik yonim*, 'your eyes [are] doves,' here and in poem 15 as an ellipsis for 'your eyes are like the eyes of doves.' KJV reflects this interpretation with 'thou hast doves' eyes' but modern versions do not: RSV, NAB, and JB all read 'your eyes are doves.' Rabin argues that, in Arabic literature, doves were noted for their sentimental eyes, and the Hebrew intends the same point. He further demonstrates that such a reading is not ungrammatical:

As for *'enayik yonim = 'enayik kᵉyonim = 'enayik kᵉ'ene yonim*, both omission of the *k-* and omission of the *nismak* (head word of genitive relation) are perhaps not common features of Biblical Hebrew, but quite well attested . . . . For instances of comparison without *k-*, see Zephania 3:3, Jeremiah 4:26, Job 8:9. For omission of *nismak*, see Ezra 10:13, Psalms 19:10, Jeremiah 10:10, etc.

My translation reflects this interpretation visually by use of the apostrophe — 'your eyes, like doves' ' — while leaving the heard image ambiguous, as it is in the Hebrew. The case is somewhat different in poem 19, where the male beloved's eyes are compared to doves. The extended metaphor there makes difficult the reading 'eyes like eyes of doves,' and it is probable that the image in 19 is not an ellipsis as we have here.

The imagery in the last third of the poem is of a metaphorical home outdoors. This is suggested by the word *ra'ananah* which today means 'fresh' but Biblically meant 'green.' The lovers' 'bed' is probably a bed of leaves, as I have made explicit in lines 9-10 of the English; similarly, their 'rafters' are images suggested by the branches of cedar and juniper trees. The cedars of the Bible were large, broad trees (see their use as an image of grandeur in poem 19) which spread rafter-like boughs above the lovers. Another translator who makes this interpretation explicit is James Moffatt in *A New Translation of the Bible*, rev. ed. (New York: Harper Brothers, 1935), p. 743:

> Our bed of love is the green sward,
> our roof-beams are yon cedar-boughs,
> our rafters are the firs.

The concluding two lines of the poem may be the speech of both voices or of the woman alone; the Hebrew grammar leaves this ambiguous. However, line 6 of the Hebrew is related both to the previous line (with the repetition of the particle *'ap*) and to the following lines (because of the word *'arsenu*, which is parallel to *batteynu* and *rahitenu*). This suggests that lines 5-8 are the continuous speech of a single speaker, and I have therefore rendered them all as part of the woman's speech.

Poem 7
Like poem 4, poem 7 has a developed argument which culminates in the affirmation of the I-Thou relataionship. Unlike 4, 7 is a dialogue, and the love relationship unfolds in a short sequence of statements and responses.

The key to this poem's meaning lies in the interpretation of the plant imagery. The controversial *h°basselet hassaron* and *sosannat ha'maqim* of the opening stanza, translated in KJV as 'rose of Sharon' and 'lily of the valley,' are, in the opinion of Nogah Hareuveni, director of Neot Kedumim, the *tulipa sharonensis* and *narcissus tazetta*. (These and other identifications of flora and fauna by Hareuveni are from personal conversation with him and correspondence with his assistant, Helen Frenkley, May-July, 1972.) While the former grows in sandy parts of the plains and the latter in a variety of habitats, the two share the feature of being common wildflowers. The point of the female speaker's identification of herself with these two flowers, then, may be that she grows like a wildflower in any number of locales. The male speaker, on the other hand, says that to him, she is unique, a single *šošannah*, 'narcissus,' brightest of all flowers; next to her, all others seem like brambles. She then rejoins with a similar compliment, calling him a fruit-bearing tree in an otherwise fruitless thicket; the Hebrew *ya'ar*, as Hareuveni points out, could not have meant a forest as we think of one today, but something smaller, like a thicket. In the protective shade of his embrace, the female speaker more than grows: she blossoms (literally, 'delights') and tastes the sweetness of his fruit, a metaphorical statement of the erotic experience. The specific fruit tree mentioned in the second stanza of the Hebrew, *tappuaḥ*, is usually mistranslated 'apple.' Today we know that apples did not grow in Biblical Palestine, and, as Hareuveni suggests, the *tappuaḥ* may have been a quince. Thus in poems 8, 23, and 27, I translate *tappuaḥ* 'quince' or 'quince tree,' but here, where it is a metaphor for the male beloved, I render it 'sweet fruit tree,' to emphasize the erotic associations.

The poem thus proceeds by association, with the mutual exchange of praises becoming more emphatic as the dialogue progresses, until it ends on a note of silent union.

Poem 8

The second line of this poem presents a semantic difficulty with the word *diglo*, usually taken to mean 'flag, OR banner.' KJV reads, 'his banner over me was love' but this interpretation does not make much sense in context. I understand *diglo* to be related to the Akkadian root *dagalu*, 'glance,' and thus read the line to mean literally, 'his glance upon me was love,' and translate it 'gazing at me with love.' Meek (IB, p. 113) points out that this root is assumed in several versions (Septuagint, Symmachus, Old Latin, Syriac, and Arabic) but they vocalize as an imperative: 'look at me with love.' I assume the same root for two difficult words in poems 19 and 20. Thus I read *dagul* in poem 19 as 'seen,' that is, visible or outstanding among many, and render it there as 'radiant' (line 25 of the English). In poem 20, I translate the difficult *nidgalot*, which appears in the third and the last lines of the Hebrew, as 'visions,' that is, something apprehended by sight. This is in contrast to the rather odd 'army with banners,' offered in KJV and RSV.

The ending of poem 8 is almost identical to the endings of poems 13 and 25: all three poems close with the adjuration to the city women, although in the Hebrew poem 25 this adjuration is somewhat abbreviated (the reference to the does is omitted). My interpretation of the oath administered to the city women differs from the standard versions. Literally, the last two lines of the oath are, 'Do not waken, do not arouse love until it desires, OR is satisfied.' Most versions read this as an admonition not to arouse passion prematurely; thus, RSV translates: 'that you stir not up nor awaken love until it please.' But why, in the context of these poems, should a female speaker warn the city women not to arouse their own, or their lovers', passion? KJV senses the incongruity and translates: 'that ye stir not up, nor awaken my love, till he please.' But this too is an improbable reading, since nowhere else in the Song is the male beloved referred to by the word *'ahabah*, 'love' (which is feminine in gender). NEB tries to solve the problem by assigning the lines to a male speaker: 'Do not rouse her, do not disturb my love until she is ready,' but this assignation is highly unlikely. I read this line to mean, 'Do not waken, do not rouse us (the lovers) until we are satisified'; that is, 'Do not rouse us from our lovemaking until we are ready to be disturbed.' Hence my translation: 'Not to wake or rouse us / Till we fulfill our love.'

Poems 8 and 25 also have in common the wistful couplet — 'O for his arms around me, / Beneath me and above' — which precedes the adjuration, and which, like it, seems formulaic. This couplet expresses fantasy rather than reality, projecting a hypothetical situation in the future. Thus, the speaker first imagines the love embrace, then warns the city women not to disturb it. This reading is supported by the fact that in the only other instance where the same adjuration appears, poem 13, it follows another fantasy — this time, of the woman grabbing and holding her lover (she is the embracer here, as he was in 8 and 25) until she has led him from the street back to the shelter of her mother's bedroom. The adjuration thus seems to express the anxiety that underlies the woman's fantasies in her lover's absence.

Poem 9

'Tender grape' in line 19 of the English is a translation of *sᵉmadar*, a difficult word which appears three times in the Song and nowhere else in the Bible. In poem 11 the same word is rendered 'new grapes'; in poem 24 I have translated it 'tender buds.' The controversy over whether to take *sᵉmadar* to refer to the early fruit or to the blossom of the grapevine does not seem to me crucial. The point is that it suggests newness and vulnerability, being either the flower or the early, hence tender, fruit.

Zamir, 'songbird' in line 16 of the English, is another controversial word. Many take *zamir* to mean 'pruning,' and *'et hazzamir* 'the pruning season' (see Meek's citations in IB, p. 116). This interpretation is unlikely because the poem is a spring song, and spring is not the time for pruning. In the Gezer Calendar, a Palestinian document from the tenth century B.C.E. (trans. W. F. Albright in Pritchard, p. 320), there is evidence that *zmr* refers to a summer agricultural activity, perhaps thinning of the vines, but this meaning too would be out of context here. Others see *zamir* as deriving from the root meaning 'song,' and render *'et hazzamir* as 'the time of singing': so translates RSV, while KJV specifies 'the time of singing of birds.' There is yet another possibility, suggested by Hareuveni: the *zamir,* he claims, is the nightingale, whose mating season, that is, the time when it sings, is in the spring. Thus *'et hazzamir* would refer to the time of year when the nightingale is heard, which is springtime. This interpretation makes sense not only because the time is right but because *'et hazzamir* 'the season of the nightingale,' is in parallel position to *qol hattor,* 'the sound of the turtledove.' I translate the two images together as 'dove and songbird singing.'

Poem 10
The final couplet of the English introduces words and images not in the Hebrew. The Hebrew states, literally, 'Your voice [is] pleasant, your appearance [is] lovely.' I have rendered 'appearance' as 'body,' to add concreteness. Because adjectives like *'areb,* 'pleasant,' and *naweh,* 'lovely,' (and others found elsewhere in the Song, such as *yapeh,* 'pretty, OR nice-looking' and *tob* 'good, OR sweet'), which are frequent in Biblical Hebrew, tend to fall flat in English, I have tried to render them more evocatively in the poems. Here I turned one into an image: 'Your voice clear as water.' The image of water seemed right, consonant with both the landscape and the emotional context of the poem, and with the imagery of the Song as a whole: elsewhere in the Song, water flows from the mountains and is associated with the female beloved. (See, for example, poem 18 and the comments on it.)

One might ask why it should be necessary to introduce specific images into the English if the Hebrew verse works without them. It is difficult to say exactly how the Hebrew manages to incorporate so many 'flat' adjectives without itself becoming flat verse. Perhaps one explanation is the musical quality of the original, which sustains many of the lines. The repetition of vowel patterns in the closing couplet of this poem adds to the structural effect of the chiastic parallelism.[3] Because this assonance could not be preserved in translation, I felt that some other poetic effect was needed to compensate, and I chose, in this case, to add imagery.

Poem 11

Although puzzling, this poem is not totally opaque. As discussed in the previous chapter, the vineyards ('vines' in my translation) seem to represent female sexuality in this poem; note too that they are described here as being in the vulnerable stage of $s^e madar$, 'early blossoming, OR new fruit.' The foxes may be young men, hostile invaders like the city guards in poem 19. As we have seen, danger lurks in the background of several poems in the Song; this poem in particular seems to be a mood piece which emphasizes the threatening undercurrents of the collection.

Poem 12

The opening two lines of the English are an expansion of the tightly compressed Hebrew line *dodi li wa'^{a}ni lo*, literally, 'My lover [is] to me and I [am] to him.' KJV, RSV, and NJPS all translate, 'My beloved is mine, and I am his,' indicating a passive state of possession. But the preposition l^e-, 'to,' may imply more: it may be an ellipsis for a verb of action. I see the opening lines not as a statement of passive possession but as an assertion of mutual, active choice, and to suggest that I introduce a verb, one which suggests both physical and emotional movement: 'My lover turns to me, / I turn to him.' Similarly, in poem 19 I translate *'^{a}ni l^{e}dodi w^{e}dodi li*, literally, 'I [am] to my lover and my lover [is] to me,' as 'I turn to meet my love, / He'll turn to me.' In poem 24, the opening line, *'^{a}ni l^{e}dodi w^e'alay t^{e}šuqato*, literally, 'I [am] to my lover and for, OR toward, me [is] his desire,' reads in my version,

---

[3] Chiasmus (from the Greek *chi*, X) refers to parallelisms in which the elements of a line are reversed in a subsequent line, as for example, A B / B A . In this case, the Hebrew lines, translated literally, can be analyzed as follows:

   A   B   C   D
Show me your *appearance* / Let me hear your **voice** //
          D   E   B   F
For your **voice** is pleasant / And your *appearance* is lovely
A *B* / C **D** // **D** E / *B* F

'Turning to him, who meets me with desire —.' Thus, in all three cases, I take the preposition *l^e-* to imply a preceding verb of movement. These lines may have been variations on a convention, for they are remarkably similar in syntax and meaning, and I repeat the verbs 'turn' and 'meet' in the three English poems in order to emphasize this similarity.

The closing line of the Hebrew poem is sometimes emended to read *'al hare b^esamim,* 'on the mountains of spices,' to agree with the last line of poem 31, where I translate 'On the fragrant hills.' (For a list of these emendations, see the critical apparatus in BH, p. 1203; also Gordis, p. 83.) Emendation here is unnecessary. The image as given, *hare bater,* 'split, OR cut, mountains,' is a vivid geographical description, probably quite accurate. According to Hareuveni, the word *beter* refers to a geological cut and aptly describes the mountains in the Galil, which look split. Thus, I translate 'in the clefts of the hills.' This image, moreover, has appropriate erotic overtones. Although I believe that the main thrust of the statement is 'go away now — come back later,' there is a concurrent symbolic reading. The deer and the hills, erotic metaphors for the man and woman, foreshadow the love relationship later to be fulfilled.

Poem 13

This poem of search-for-the-beloved exemplifies the initiative often assumed by female speakers in the Song. One is struck by the persistence of the speaker, culminating in her unabashed declaration, 'I won't let him go.' Here, as in poem 25, the speaker announces her intention to bring her lover to her mother's home, where she will be free to pursue the love relationship. Again, as in poem 25, this poem concludes with an adjuration to the city women not to invade the privacy of the home.

As already observed, this poem is in the mode of a fantasy; in fact, because the speech begins 'in bed,' the events which follow may be seen as parts of a dream, although if so, the dream is less obvious here than in poem 19, where the speaker actually says she is asleep. I tried to preserve the dreamlike sense of time in this poem by interweaving present and future tenses in the English.

Poem 14

The resonances of the opening line of the Hebrew are difficult to convey in translation. The verb *'olah* means 'rise,' and is used in the

Bible to express many kinds of ascension, both physical and spiritual. It often has religious meaning, as in the sacrificial rites, literally, 'offerings up,' in Leviticus and elsewhere. Journeys to Jerusalem are also referred to by this verb, and in this poem *'olah* seems to mean 'ascending toward Jerusalem' from the wilderness. It was difficult to preserve in English the religious and ritualistic overtones of the movement suggested by *'olah*; and I settled for 'approaching, up from the wilderness.' It is also unclear how much religious resonance was intended in this Hebrew poem, but one senses a grand, even awesome atmosphere here, more so than in most other poems in the collection. I tried to preserve some of this effect in English by creating a formal poem of long rhyming lines and elevated diction.

The imagery of the opening stanza was also a challenge to translate. 'Incense' in line 2 of the English is a descriptive rendering of the two words *mor* and *lᵉbonah*, literally, 'myrrh' and 'frankincense' in the Hebrew line 3. I avoided literal translations of both these words because of their now dominant association with the Christian Nativity, an anachronistic and inappropriate association for the Song. The point of these images in the Song is their fragrance; hence, I translated them as 'incense' in this poem, as 'fragrant bloom' in the penultimate stanza of 15, and as 'fragrant woods' and 'perfumes' in the fourth stanza of poem 18.

The role of the mother in this poem is also rather unusual. Elsewhere she is associated with the home and with sites for lovemaking; in poem 25 she is the one who 'teaches' love. Here she plays a more formal role, crowning the king on his wedding day. Samuel Noah Kramer speculates that this passage is a late reflection of an ancient Hebrew 'Sacred Marriage Rite' in *The Sacred Marriage Rite* (Bloomington: Indiana Univ. Press, 1969), p. 90. However, the crown need not be royal; it may refer to the headpiece worn in marriage ceremonies. As Gordis (p. 84) argues: 'Crowns were worn even by ordinary grooms and brides, until the defeats sustained in the War against Rome in 70, when they were abandoned as a sign of mourning (cf. B. Sotah 49a).' It is fitting that the mother, who implicitly supports lovemaking elsewhere, officially sanctions it here.

Poem 15

The body of this poem is a *wasf*, whose features are discussed in chapter four. Here I discuss the frame of the poem, that is, the relationship between its opening and closing lines.

The poem opens with the exclamation *hinnak yapah ra^{e}yati*, literally, 'behold, you are fair, my beloved' ('How fine / you are, my love' in my translation), and proceeds to describe various parts of the beloved's body. The opening three lines in the Hebrew duplicate those which open the Hebrew poem 6. So too the penultimate stanza of the Hebrew begins with two lines found elsewhere in the Song, poem 12, lines 3-4: *'ad seyapuaḥ hayyom / w^{e}nasu haṣṣ^{e}lalim* (translated in my poem 15 as 'Until / the day is over, / shadows gone'). These lines lead into the speaker's resolution to take himself away to the hills. The speaker's concluding words, which follow this resolution, return to a description of the beloved. The exclamation of the penultimate line, *kullak yapah ra^{e}yati*, literally, 'all of you is fair, my beloved,' is an echo of the opening line, but more emphatic. The *waṣf* in the poem is thus framed by what seem to be conventional expressions, that is, phrases that may have been the common stock of oral poets. In fact, the incompleteness of the *waṣf* and the reappearance of part of it in poem 20 give some reason to think that the entire poem was fashioned from conventional bits and pieces, by a poet or possibly a compiler. Nonetheless, the poem as we now have it stands on its own, as a well-framed love monologue praising the beloved.

Poem 16

The Hebrew poem is open to at least two different interpretations, based on different readings for the verb *taš̌uri* in line 3 of both the Hebrew and English poems. *Taš̌uri* has at least two distinct meanings: either 'to descend,' as in Isaiah 57:9 and Exekiel 27:25, or 'to see, behold, regard,' as in Numbers 23:9. Thus the third line of the Hebrew, *taš̌uri mero'š '^{a}manah*, may mean either 'descend from the top of Amana' or 'look [down] from the top of Amana.' KJV reads 'look from the top of Amana'; RSV gives 'depart from the peak of Amana' but cites 'look' as an alternative for 'depart.' I choose the meaning 'come down' in the third line of my translation, but incorporate both meanings in the poem's last line, 'Look down, look down and come away!' Thus the situation of the poem is this: The woman is in the mountains, the speaker somewhere below. He calls her attention to him and invites her to join him, attempting to persuade her that her present environment, aside from being distant from him, is too dangerous a place for her to stay.

Poem 17

The much-discussed appellation, 'my sister, my bride,' appears twice in this poem, and twice again in poem 18. It is by now a commonplace to note that the Egyptians used 'sister' as an endearing term and that the Hebrews did the same.[4] The modern reader especially should have no difficulty reading the terms 'sister' and 'bride' as metaphors. Just as it is inappropiate to read 'sister' as 'sibling' here, it is unnecessary to read 'bride' as significantly different from 'beloved'; the poem does not seem to be about marital love any more than about a sibling relationship.

Note that in poem 25 there is another, this time hypothetical reference to a sibling relationship. The female speaker there claims that *if* her beloved were actually her brother, she would feel free to kiss him in public. This testifies to the intimacy presumably allowed to siblings in this culture, which the speakers in poems 17 and 18 wish to evoke.

Elsewhere in the text, such as in poems 2 and 29, sibling relationships seem to be real rather than metaphorical, and fraught with conflict. These different meanings reflect a diversity of attitudes and situations among siblings, which is not surprising for a collection of various types of poems. Moreover, it is understandable that real familial relationships may be less ideal than hypothetical or metaphorical ones. The relationships in poems 2 and 29 are perhaps more difficult to interpret than the reference to 'sister-bride' in poems 17 and 18, or than the string of endearments, including the term 'my sister,' in poem 19, but the difficulties in poems 2 and 29 need not complicate our understanding of the endearing terms in 17, 18, and 19.

Poem 18

Coming at almost the midpoint of the text is the archetypal 'garden poem,' in which the extended metaphor of the garden governs from beginning to end. The garden here functions equally as a metaphor for the beloved and as the setting where the lovers meet. The speaker

---

[4] See, for example, 'The Love Songs and the Song of the Harper,' trans. Simpson in Simpson, ed., pp. 296-325. The following quotations are from love songs of the New Kingdom. From love poems spoken by a woman (pp. 302-303): 'My brother, my loved one, / my heart chases after your love' and 'Now must I depart from the brother, / and [as I long] for your love, / my heart stands still inside me.' From a love poem spoken by a man (p. 310): 'The love of my sister lies on yonder side.'

addresses his beloved as a garden; she replies, referring to 'my garden' (myself, my sexuality) which then becomes in the Hebrew 'his garden'; finally he speaks of '*my* garden,' implying that he has entered and is already within. The garden is described as lush with flowers, spices, and fruits, and eating and drinking are central erotic motifs. Images of water are also central: the whole garden as a metaphor for the beloved is parallel to the pool and the fountain in the opening lines. Later, the beloved is referred to as a fountain, a well of living water, flowing streams. While water seems to be the substance that nurtures all the plants *in* the garden (the Hebrew *ma‘eyan gannim* in line 10 means 'fountain of gardens'), as another metaphor for the beloved it is also *equivalent to* the garden.

One cannot unravel the interwoven layers of symbolic meaning in the poem without rending the fabric of the whole. The poem seems to depend on a special kind of logic which is appropriate for expressing the existential paradoxes of the love relationship. It operates like this: Because I am nourished by my beloved, who satisfies my desires, my beloved is my garden. But since she possesses all the pleasurable qualities of water, flowers, fruits, and spices, she is also all those things *in* the garden. Thus she herself is located *in* the garden, and I enter the symbolic garden on both levels. I am *with* her, inside the place she inhabits, and *in* her, inside her self. And thus I experience the paradox of union in love, of two distinct selves — the I and the Thou — becoming one and yet remaining two.

The two-as-one experience of the I-Thou relationship is at the core of all the love dialogues. In this poem it finds expression in a complex extended metaphor that has come to represent ideal love in the Western tradition. (Edwin M. Good offers an insightful analysis of the garden as an extended mataphor in this poem in his article, 'Ezekiel's Ship: Some Extended Metaphors in the Old Testament,' *Semitics*, 1 [1970], 93-97.)

It makes sense then to read the closing exclamation as the voice of a third speaker or speakers who stand outside the love relationship and address the lovers. In contrast, to read the line as an invitation to other friends by one of the lovers violates grotesquely the metaphor of the garden as an enclosed and private world-of-two.

Poem 19
Because this poem is so much longer and structurally more complex than the others in the collection, it has been treated extensively in the

preceding chapters. Here I add comments on two idiomatic Hebrew phrases.

Line 12 of the Hebrew, *ume'ay hamu 'alaw*, is literally, 'And my bowels churned, OR rumbled, for him.' Phyllis Trible suggests that *me'ay* means 'womb' (*God and the Rhetoric of Sexuality* [Philadelphia: Fortress Press, 1978], p. 45), but the usual reading of the line is figurative. For the ancient Hebrews, the bowels were the seat of the emotions; the closest equivalent in English is the heart; hence, my translation: 'and my heart leaps for him!' (line 10 of the English).

Line 19 of the Hebrew, *napšiyaṣe'ah bedabbero* (the first part of line 14 in the English: 'I run out after him, . . . '), means literally, 'My soul went out upon his speaking, OR with his words.' Meek suggests 'My soul went forth upon his speaking' or 'upon his turning away,' and interprets this to mean 'I fainted when he spoke' or 'I fainted when he turned away' (IB, p. 128). But there may be a better reading. As the narrative is recorded in a state of semiconsciousness, semidreaming, the 'soul' may be a figure for the self and 'his speaking' a figure for the beloved: thus, *'I run after him.'* The actions which ensue are searching and calling out for the beloved. It hardly seems likely that the speaker would rush into such frenzied activity immediately after fainting, and it is better to read the idiom as the beginning of a continued pursuit of the beloved. To convey this, I have compressed lines 19-21 of the Hebrew into a single English line: 'I run out after him, calling, but he is gone.'

Poem 20

This poem looks somewhat like four fragments, and one might maintain that it is not a coherent poetic unit. I would argue, however, that these fragments, which I treat as stanzas, seem to accrue resonance from each other, together forming a powerful statement of praise for the beloved. The motif of seeing, which recurs in each of the stanzas, effectively links them together and suggests that they constitute a single poetic whole.

The first stanza opens with an exclamation of awe at the sight of the beloved, who is compared to two capital cities, Tirza in the northern kingdom and Jerusalem in Judea. The problematic word in the stanza is *nidgalot*, a form appearing twice in this poem but nowhere else in the Bible, and usually translated 'army with banners,' from the root *dgl*, meaning 'flag.' This reading makes little sense in context; it is better to read *nidgalot* to mean 'visions,' from the Akkadian *dagalu*, meaning 'glance' (cf. *diglo* in poem 8 and *dagul* in poem 19, discussed in the note to poem 8). Gordis also argues for this reading of *nidgalot* (pp. 90-92), accounting for the feminine plural suffix of the word in the first stanza by reference to the cities of Tirza and Jerusalem, and in the fourth stanza by reference to the heavenly bodies. The first stanza ends with the speaker's admonition to his beloved to avert her eyes, for her gaze makes him tremble.

The second stanza is a fragment of the *wasf* found in poem 15. Referring back to poem 15, from which these lines are repeated almost exactly, we see that there the preceding image was of the beloved's eyes. Similarly, the image of eyes at the end of the first stanza of this poem leads into the descriptions of hair, teeth, and forehead which comprise the second stanza.

In the third stanza, the beloved is highlighted against a context of queens, concubines (my translation of *pilagšim* as 'brides' is a concession made for the sake of English verse), and young women. She alone stands out, unique and special, like the 'narcissus in the brambles' of poem 7. To the eye of her mother, she is *barah*, 'pure'; so too she appears to the young women, who, like the speaker of the poem, praise her upon seeing her beauty.

The word *barah* links the third and fourth stanzas, and we see from the fourth stanza that the connotations of this word too are visual. An alternate meaning of *barah* is 'bright'; I tried to preserve this sense by using 'bright' for the translation of *yapah* (literally, 'pretty, OR nice-looking') in the preceding parallel line. The woman herself becomes a cosmic figure, staring down from the heavens, bright, literally 'pretty,' as the moon and pure-bright as the sun. *Šaḥar*, literally 'dawn,' may refer to the morning star, Venus, or to the sun itself (note the association with the sun in poem 2); I translate it 'dawn's eye.' Here, as in poem 2, celestial globes are depicted as staring eyes, and the motif of vision is thus sustained throughout the last stanza.

There is a bold, almost primitive quality about this last stanza. The words for moon and sun are not the usual *yareaḥ* and *šemeš*, but the more vivid *lᵉbanah*, whose root means 'white,' and *ḥamah*, whose root means 'hot.' I make these associations explicit in the translations 'white moon' and 'hot sun.' The awesome tone of this stanza harks back to the mood of the opening stanza; both stanzas close with the striking *nidgalot*, 'visions.' The appearance of this unusual word twice in one poem now seems highly purposeful: more than an inclusion (a rhetorical device which provides an outer frame), *nidgalot* pulls together the internal motif of seeing which has recurred in various ways.

If the four stanzas of this poem were not originally composed together, they were probably placed side by side by a skillful compiler. The poem as it stands conveys the thrill of gazing upon the beloved, whose own glance is as powerful as the sun's.

Poem 21

'The signs of spring' (line 2 of the English) is an interpretation of *'ibbe hannaḥal,* literally, 'fruits of the valley, OR of the riverbed.' Hareuveni suggests that the word *'ibbe* may refer to reeds, *'ibbubim,* which, like walnut trees, grow near streams. The reeds appear in the spring season, at the time of the flowering of the vines and pomegranate trees. The word *'ibbe* may also be related to *'abib,* a springtime month or the first stage of ripening.

Chapter 6, verse 12 of the Hebrew, which is presented in the reconstruction of the Hebrew set apart from poem 21, is the only line in the text that I have not rendered into English. I find it impossible to propose even a literal translation of this hopelessly garbled line; almost everyone agrees that, as it stands, it is unintelligible. Meek states flatly, 'This is the one hopelessly corrupt verse in the Song' (IB, p. 134). KJV translates it as follows: 'Or ever I was aware, my soul made me like the chariots of Ammi-nadib.' RSV does not improve much upon the sense: 'Before I was aware, my fancy set me in a chariot beside my prince.' Recently some ingenious attempts have been made to render sense out of ostensible nonsense here, but so much emendation is involved that the original words hardly remain intact. See, for example, Gordis' commentary, pp. 92-93. Based in part on an emendation proposed by Tur-Sinai, Gordis translates this verse (p. 67): 'I am beside myself with joy, / For there wilt thou give me thy myrrh, / O noble kinsman's daughter!' Gordis refers in his commentary to other proposed emendations as well. I agree with Meek that 'any restoration is a guess, and although many have been offered there is none that is satisfactory' (IB, p. 134). Moreover, even if we alter the line to make grammatical sense, it still has little meaning in context. Therefore, admitting defeat, I omit this line from my translation.

Poem 22

This poem is the only complete *wasf* in the Song which describes a female figure. The most difficult images to visualize in this *wasf* are those based on natural and architectural phenomena set in particular places. The eyes are like pools in Heshbon, at the gates of Bat-Rabbim; the nose, or, as I interpret it, face, is like the tower of Lebanon overlooking Damascus; the head is like Mount Carmel. Heshbon was a city located east of the Dead Sea; Damascus was, as now, the capital of Syria; Carmel was and is a mountain on the Mediterranean coast, north of present-day Haifa. Because these names no longer carry the resonance they once had, I deleted them from the translation and referred instead to the visual associations of these places. Thus the eyes are like pools, languid, or large and reflective; the face is a tower that surveys its surroundings; the head has a commanding height, a majestic quality carried through in the regal imagery of the last two lines.

The word *'appek*, which I translate 'your face,' is translated 'your nose' in most other versions, producing the troublesome image of a towering nose. There are several reasons, besides aesthetic preference, to read 'face' here. First, the parts of the anatomy are described in this passage, as in the other complete *wasf* in poem 19, in a linear progression, in this case from bottom to top. There is in fact a strict adherence here to the order of the sequence: none of the parts is out of place. It follows that between the descriptions of the eyes and the head we are not given a description of the nose but of the general picture of the face. Secondly, *'ap* seems to mean 'face' in other Biblical passages as well, for example, Genesis 3:19. Thirdly, a face, but not a nose, may be described by the verb which follows, *ṣopeh*, 'scouting,' in the sense of 'looking out' or, as I suggest in my translation, 'overlooking.' Finally, we see that the neck too is described in this poem as a tower. A towerlike neck implies length and grandeur, but a towerlike nose seems especially ridiculous following so closely upon the description of the neck. Is the nose being compared in size or stature to the neck? Surely not. Rather, the image of the face is a continuation of the image of the neck: as the neck is long and stately, the face is elevated and looking forth from its height. The sense of elevation or grandeur is then consummated by the description of the head and hair — mountainlike, majestic, able to capture a king.

The word *šor°rek*, usually rendered 'your navel,' is also difficult. It probably refers to the vulva, coming as it does in sequence after the description of the thighs and before the belly. According to Meek (IB, p. 135), the Arabic cognate of the word suggests this reading. Because English has no word that is not either clinical or pornographic in tone,

I regretfully had to circumlocute and render the image as 'hips.' Still, 'hips' has more erotic associations than 'navel,' and the conjunction of 'hips' with 'bowl of nectar' I hope suggests the image more clearly than the standard translations.

The word *šulammit* in the first line of the Hebrew, usually given in English as a transliterated proper name, 'Shulammite,' is controversial. Some suggest it derives from the name Solomon (so Meek, IB, pp. 134–135); others emend to Shunammite, woman of Shunem, the domicile of Abishag (I Kings 1:3). H. H. Rowley summarizes the many different interpretations of this word in 'The Meaning of "The Shulammite," ' *American Journal of Semitic Languages and Literatures*, 56 (1930), 84–91; none seems to me entirely convincing. I therefore chose not to confuse the English poem with an enigmatic proper name, and instead translated the word as 'princess,' taking my cue from *bat-nadib*, 'daughter of nobility,' another appellation for the woman given a few lines later in the Hebrew. As the poem culminates with regal imagery, it is likely that regality is suggested also at the outset.

The dance being watched is given a curious name in the Hebrew: *meḥolat hammaḥᵃnayim*. It may be the dance of a particular place, Mahanayim, referred to in Genesis 32:3; or it may be understood as 'dance of two camps' from *maḥᵃneh*, 'camp.' RSV renders 'dance before two armies.' The meaning of the phrase is uncertain, but it seems to refer to a performance before a group of people, and the description itself leads one to think of belly-dancing, probably in the nude.

Poem 23

'Clusters of dates' in line 4 of the English is a translation of *'aškolot* in line 4 of the Hebrew, literally, 'clusters.' KJV assumes 'clusters of grapes,' but this is not consonant with the figure of the palm tree. Furthermore, in line 7, the Hebrew specifies *'eškᵉlot haggepen*, 'clusters of the vine,' for a deliberate and purposeful shift of imagery. It is at this point that the portrait changes from that of a stately palm tree to a free-flowing sequence of disconnected images, parts of imagined experience: your breasts will be like clusters of the vine, that is, soft as grapes; your breath will be like quinces; your palate like wine.

The closing lines of the poem in Hebrew are among the most difficult in the text. Literally, they are, 'Your palate is like good wine / Going to my beloved (masculine) smoothly, OR like new wine, / Gliding over, OR stirring, the lips of sleepers.' *Lᵉmešarim*, 'smoothly,

OR like new wine,' is a difficult form; *dobeb*, 'gliding, OR stirring,' is a *hapax legomenon*. *Dodi*, the term for the male beloved, is out of place here because a man speaks this poem to a woman, and it is therefore emended by many to *dodim*, 'lovers.' NEB reads *doday*, 'my caresses.' *Śipte yᵉśenim*, 'lips of sleepers,' makes little sense and is emended by the Septuagint, Aquila, and Syriac to 'my lips and teeth'; the Vulgate gives 'his lips and teeth'; others read 'lips and teeth' (as cited by Meek, IB, p. 39). NAB and NEB follow the last emendation and translate 'lips and teeth.' None of the proposed emendations for these difficult words and phrases help the sense very much; hence my translation does not assume any of these readings but is essentially a free reworking of the basic ideas and images: 'Like wine that entices / The lips of new lovers.'

Poem 24

For discussion of the opening line, see the note to poem 12.

Kᵉparim in line 3 of the Hebrew is usually translated 'villages,' but it can also mean 'henna,' as I render it in line 3 of the English. *Koper*, 'henna,' appears elsewhere in the text, in the Hebrew poem 5, line 5 (where I translate it 'blossoms' in line 7 of the English), and makes good sense in the flowering environment here. NJPS also translates 'henna' here.

The movement of 'returning' (line 9 of the English) is not stated explicitly in the Hebrew, but is suggested by the shift of contexts from the countryside to the home, and by the implied passage of time.

Poem 25

Grammatically, *tᵉlammᵉdeni* (line 7 of the Hebrew, line 6 of the English) can mean either 'she teaches me' or 'you (masculine) teach me.' I read the former, the referent being 'my mother.'

As I mentioned in the note to poem 8, the closing adjuration of this poem is here abbreviated in the Hebrew, the second line being omitted. There is, however, some weak textual evidence for the complete adjuration here in four Hebrew manuscripts and the Greek and Arabic versions. (See BH, p. 1210.) Mainly to emphasize the similarities in the three poems where the adjuration occurs (poems 8, 13, and 25), and to call attention to its formulaic nature, I have translated it identically each time.

Poem 26
This poem seems to be a fragment, the first line of the Hebrew (two lines in English) being an exact duplication of the opening line of poem 14. While it constitutes only half of a Biblical verse, it is not related thematically to the second half, and I saw no way of uniting the two half-verses.

Poem 27
This short three-line poem in Hebrew constitutes the second half of a Biblical verse, yet it stands on its own as a poetic unit. While many commentators assume a man speaks this poem, it is a masculine singular 'you' which is addressed, strongly indicating a female speaker.

The word *ḥibbᵉlatᵉka*, which I translate 'conceived,' is a verbal form of the root *ḥbl*, which usually refers to labor in childbirth. Thus KJV translates, 'there thy mother brought thee forth.' According to KB (p. 271), the Syriac cognate of the word can mean either 'to conceive' or 'to bear.' In Psalms 7:15, *yᵉḥabbel* is the first in a progression of three verbs, the others being *harah*, 'be pregnant,' and *yalad*, 'give birth.' The order of the verbs here seems to suggest that *yᵉḥabbel* means 'conceive' rather than 'bear,' and the meaning 'conceive' fits poem 27 as well. The speaker suggests that the place where she aroused her beloved is also the place where his mother made love. As we have seen in other poems, the outdoor country setting is conducive to lovemaking, and the figure of the mother also supports erotic atmosphere. The mother's own erotic experience under the quince tree is mentioned as stimulation for, perhaps even legitimization of, the present lovemaking. The mention of labor pains would hardly seem to be as effective.

Poem 28
The tone of this Hebrew poem is unlike that of any other in the collection. The strong synonymous parallelisms, the extensive use of alliteration, and the sweeping images of fire and water all contribute to the powerful mood. There are those who assume a male speaker here, but the pronominal suffixes indicate a woman speaking, and nothing in the poem contradicts this.

The opening lines are literally, 'Put me like a seal on your heart / Like a seal on your arm,' and are often understood as a reference to amulets worn on the chest or arm. The seal may have been a sign of ownership (cf. Genesis 38:18), but this meaning, as we shall see, is inappropriate here and is directly negated by the poem's ending. In keeping with the fiery imagery of the poem, I have translated to the stronger image of an emblem pressed or seared into the flesh. So too the *Zohar*, the central work of Kabbalah, comments: ' "Set me as a seal upon thy heart." For, as the imprint of the seal is to be discerned even after the seal is withdrawn, so I shall cling to you.' (Gershom Scholem, ed., *Zohar: The Book of Splendor* [New York: Schocken, 1963], p. 70).

The word *šalhebetyah*, which I translate 'a fierce / And holy blaze,' has an emphatic particle suffix, *-yah*, which tradition views as a reference to the name of God, the only such reference in the Song. Most translations render without any mention of God, as 'a most vehement flame' (KJV and RSV) and 'a blazing flame' (NJPS). Meek suggests 'flame of Yah,' finding the meaning 'emphatic in accordance with the Hebrew idiom of using the divine name with superlative force' (IB, p. 144). I have deliberately retained just a hint of the word's theological resonance in my translation, 'holy blaze.'

Indeed the poem has cosmic, if not religious, overtones. The *mayim rabbim*, literally, 'many, OR great, waters,' which I translate 'Endless seas and floods, / Torrents,' may be a reference to a mythical force, the waters of chaos. (See, for example, H. G. May, 'Some Cosmic Connotations of *Mayim Rabbim*, "Many Waters," ' *Journal of Biblical Literature*, 74 [1955], 9-21.) *Sᵉ'ol*, which I translate (with KJV and RSV) 'the grave,' is actually the place of the dead in Hebrew cosmology. While 'the grave' is a weak equivalent for *šᵉ'ol*, the alternatives are worse. The English 'hell' has inappropriate connotations, such as a sense of punishment, and could not be used here.

The poem closes with an aphorism, leading back from the world of myth into the realm of human mores and behavior. The Hebrew pronoun *lo* in the last line may refer either to wealth or to the buyer of love. In either case the message is the same: love cannot be bought. It is clear now that the 'seal' of the opening lines is not a sign of acquired possession; the poem as a whole argues against such a reading.

Thus, mythic vision climaxes in didactic pronouncement, suggesting the shape of a fiery sermon. But the poem is first of all a love lyric, opening with an entreaty to the beloved, and it should not be reduced to the moral lesson of its closing adage. Perhaps to avoid this risk, JB separates the last stanza and labels it an appendix, the 'Aphorism of a Sage.' But this cuts off the resolution of the speech and denies poetic closure. Rather, the poem should be seen as a complex unit which moves from an intense personal plea to a cosmic statement, and finally finds resolution in a piece of practical morality.

Poem 29

This dialogue is one of the more perplexing poems in the collection. First of all, it is difficult to say who is speaking to whom. It sounds like a chorus of older brothers (like the men who sent their sister out to tend vines in poem 2?) but grammatically it could be either men or women speaking. Another possibility is that the first stanza is spoken by the woman's brothers and the second by her suitors. I find this unlikely, however, and read both stanzas as the speech of the woman's brothers, to whom she replies in the third stanza.

The imagery too is strange. The Hebrew states baldly that the little sister 'has no breasts'; I render this imagistically, to soften the effect: 'We have a young sister / Whose breasts are but flowers.' 'If she's a wall,' the speakers say, they will build her a parapet of silver; however, 'if she's a door,' they will board her up with cedar. Besides being images for her flat chest, the wall and door seem to have other symbolic meaning. The impenetrable surface of the wall suggest chastity, while the door represents an open invitation. Thus, silver is the reward given to the woman for having kept herself chaste, whereas the plank of cedar will board her up if she has been wanton. If this reading is correct, then the brothers here are like those in poem 2, both protective and punitive.

Another reading, which I find less likely, is that the wall and the door are in synonymous parallelism, both architectural images of flatness without other connotation. In this case, the brothers would be offering to adorn their sister with two precious commodities, silver and cedar, to make her more attractive to potential suitors.

In either case, the sister's reply is adamant. She rejects their concern, stating proudly that her breasts are like towers, fully developed, at least in her own estimation. Thus, she claims, she needs no assistance from these men, for she has already found her own 'peace,' her happiness with her lover. The meaning of *moṣ'et šalom*, 'finding peace,' is similar to that of *maṣa' ḥen*, 'finding favor.' In other words, she has found favor in her lover's eyes and therefore also in her own.

Although the expression 'finding peace' may at first seem odd, it is consonant with the fortress imagery of the poem. The poem is built on the conceit of war and it concludes, fittingly, with a truce. In the battle with her brothers, the young woman emerges triumphant. Because she is her own fortress, she needs no defenders, and can make peace on her own terms.[5]

Poem 30

This poem is another difficult one whose argument is open to debate. The grammar does not specify the speaker's gender, and determining this depends largely on how one understands the symbol of the vineyard. In poem 2, the vineyard represents the woman's sexuality; there, a woman refers to her 'own' vineyard, that is, to an aspect of herself. If a similar reading pertains here, one might argue that the speaker of this poem is also a woman. But Solomon too has a vineyard here; if the vineyard means the female *self* in this poem, how can it apply to Solomon? It is better to read the vineyard here as a symbol for female *other* rather than female *self*, and to deduce from this that the speaker is a man. Woman as sexual other may be treated as a beloved (the speaker's relationship to his 'own' vineyard) or as a sexual object (Solomon's vineyard is a harem which must be kept under constant guard). Using the motif of regality as foil, the poem advocates the one-to-one I-Thou relationship and rejects the debasement of sexuality inherent in treating others as sexual objects or property.

Poem 31

With this poem we return to the garden and the world of the two lovers. Once again the theme of secret love emerges: the woman chases her beloved away lest they be caught by day, implying an invitation to him to return to her at night. There is a sort of false closure implied in this banishment; the poem, and thus the collection, actually concludes on a subtle note of anticipation. Given that the Song of Songs is a collection of lyrics — that is, a string of separate moments rather than a structured whole with beginning, middle, and end — it is fitting that it closes in expectation of the moment to come.

[5] Compare this poem with sixteenth- and seventeenth-century English love poems, both secular and religious, which use the conceit of warfare and truce as a central motif. For example, see Sir Thomas Wyatt's 'I find no peace' or John Donne's 'Batter my heart.'

KEY TO THE BIBLICAL TEXT

Poem	*Biblical Chapter and Verse*
Title	1:1
1	1:2-4
2	1:5-6
3	1:7-8
4	1:9-11
5	1:12-14
6	1:15-17
7	2:1-3
8	2:4-7
9	2:8-13
10	2:14
11	2:15
12	2:16-17
13	3:1-5
14	3:6-11
15	4:1-7
16	4:8
17	4:9-11
18	4:12-5:1
19	5:2-6:3
20	6:4-10
21	6:11*
22	7:1-6
23	7:7-10
24	7:11-14
25	8:1-4
26	8:5a
27	8:5b
28	8:6-7
29	8:8-10
30	8:11-12
31	8:13-14

* 6:12 of the Hebrew has not been translated because its meaning is not decipherable, but it has been presented in the Hebrew text on the same page as poem 21, set apart from the poem.

TRANSLITERATION

Consonants

ʾ	א	ṭ	ט			p	פ	ף
b	ב	y	י			ṣ (ts)	צ	ץ
g	ג	k	כ	ך		q	ק	
d	ד	l	ל			r	ר	
h	ה	m	מ	ם		ś	שׂ	
w	ו	n	נ	ן		š (sh)	שׁ	
z	ז	s	ס			t	ת	
ḥ (ch)	ח	ʿ	ע					

Spirant forms of ב, ג, ד, כ, פ, ת are not indicated.

Vowels

Long and short vowels are not distinguished; *sheʷa* is indicated by vowels raised above the line.

ABBREVIATIONS

The following abbreviations are used in chapter six:

BH   Rudolf Kittel, ed., *Biblia Hebraica*, 7th ed. (1951)

IB   Theophile J. Meek, 'The Song of Songs: Introduction and Exegesis' in *The Interpreter's Bible*, vol. V (1956)

JB   *The Jerusalem Bible* (1966)

KB   Koehler and Baumgartner, *Lexicon in Veteris Testamenti Libros* (1958)

KJV   *The Holy Bible* (Authorized or King James Version, 1611)

NAB   *The New American Bible* (1970)

NEB   *The New English Bible* (1970)

NJPS   *The Five Megilloth and Jonah* (new translation by the Jewish Publication Society, 1969)

RSV   *The Holy Bible* (Revised Standard Version, 1946-52)

BIBLIOGRAPHY

This bibliography includes works which are cited in the text, or which have been influential in my translation or interpretation of the Song.

Albright, W. F.
    'Archaic Survivals in the Text of Canticles.' In *Hebrew and Semitic Studies Presented to Godfrey Rolles Driver.* Ed. D. W. Thomas and W. D. McHardy. Oxford: Clarendon Press, 1963, pp. 1-7.

Auerbach, Erich.
    'Figura.' In *Scenes from the Drama of European Literature: Six Essays.* Trans. Ralph Manheim and Catherine Garvin. New York: Meridian Books, Inc., 1959, pp. 11-76.

Barfield, Owen.
    Poetic Diction: A Study in Meaning. Introd. by Howard Nemerov. 1st ed., 1928; rpt. New York: McGraw-Hill, 1964.

Berry, Wendell.
    'A Secular Pilgrimage.' *The Hudson Review,* 23 (1970), 401-424.

Bly, Robert.
    Leaping Poetry: An Idea with Poems and Translations. Boston: Beacon Press, 1975.

Bodenheimer, Friedrich Simon.
    Animal and Man in Bible Lands. Leiden: E. J. Brill, 1960.

Brooks, Cleanth.
    The Well Wrought Urn: Studies in the Structure of Poetry. New York: Harcourt, Brace & World, 1947.

Brower, Reuben A., ed.
    On Translation. New York: Oxford Univ. Press, 1966.

Brown, Francis; Driver, S. R.; and Briggs, Charles A.
    A Hebrew and English Lexicon of the Old Testament. 1st ed., 1907; corrected impression. Oxford: Clarendon Press, 1952.

Buber, Martin.
    Hasidism and Modern Man. Trans. Maurice Friedman. New York: Harper & Row, 1966.
    —— *I and Thou.* Trans. Walter Kaufmann. New York: Charles Scribner's Sons, 1970.
    —— trans. *Die Schriftwerke.* Vol IV of *Die Schrift.* Trans. Martin Buber and Franz Rosenzweig. Cologne: Jakob Hegner Verlag, 1962.

Buber, Martin, and Rosenzweig, Franz.
    Die Schrift und ihre Verdeutschung. Berlin: Schocken Verlag, 1936.

Cohen, Gerson D. &p 'The Song of Songs and the Jewish Religious Mentality.' In *The Samuel Friedland Lectures 1960-1966.* New York: Jewish Theological Seminary of America, 1966.

Cook Albert.
  The Root of the Thing: A Study of Job and The Song of Songs.
  Bloomington and London: Indiana Univ. Press, 1968.
Culley, Robert C.
  Oral Formulaic Language in the Biblical Psalms. Toronto: Univ. of
  Toronto Press, 1967.
Deutsch, Babette.
  Poetry Handbook. 2nd ed. New York: Grosset & Dunlap, 1962.
Driver, G. R.
  'Hebrew Poetic Diction.' In *Congress Volume, Copenhagen, 1953.*
  Supplements to Vetus Testamentum, vol. I. Leiden: E. J. Brill, 1953, pp.
  26-39.
Driver, S. R.
  An Introduction to the Literature of the Old Testament. New ed., 1913;
  rpt. New York: Charles Scribner's Sons, 1950.
—— *A Treatise on the Use of the Tenses in Hebrew and Some Other
  Syntactical Questions.* 3rd ed., 1892; rpt. Oxford: Clarendon Press,
  1969.
Dryden, John.
  Preface to *Ovid's Epistles, Translated by Several Hands.* London, 1680.
  In *The Works of John Dryden.* Eds. Edward Niles Hooker and H. T.
  Swedenberg, Jr. Berkeley: Univ. of California Press, 1961, vol. I, pp.
  109-119.
Eissfeldt, Otto.
  The Old Testament: An Introduction. Trans. Peter R. Ackroyd. New
  York: Harper & Row; Oxford: Basil Blackwell, 1965.
Exum, J. Cheryl.
  'A Literary and Structural Analysis of the Song of Songs.' *Zeitschrift für
  die alttestamentliche Wissenschaft,* 85 (1973), 47-79.
Feliks, Jehuda.
  Sir Hašširim: Teba' 'alilah W^e'aligoriyyah. Jerusalem: Ma'ªrib, 1974.
The Five Megilloth and Jonah: A New Translation.
  Introductions by H. L. Ginsberg. Philadelphia: The Jewish Publication
  Society of America, 1969.
Fox, Everett.
  'In the Beginning: An English Rendition of The Book of Genesis Based
  on the German Version of Martin Buber and Franz Rosenzweig.'
  Introduction by Nahum N. Glatzer. *Response,* No. 14 (Summer, 1972),
  pp. 1-159.
—— 'Technical Aspects of the Translation of Genesis of Martin Buber and
  Franz Rosenzweig.' Diss. Brandeis, 1974.
—— 'We Mean the Voice: The Buber-Rosenzweig Bible Translation.'
  Response, No. 12 (Winter, 1972), pp. 29-42.
Gerleman, Gillis.
  'Die Bildsprache des Hohenliedes und die altägyptische Kunst.' *Annual
  of the Swedish Theological Institute,* 1 (1962), 24-30.
—— *Ruth; Das Hohelied.* Biblischer Kommentar Altes Testament, vol.
  XVIII. Neukirchen-Vluyn: Neukirchener Verlag des Erviehungsvereins,
  1965.

Gevirtz, Stanley.
    Patterns in the Early Poetry of Israel. The Oriental Institute of Chicago
    Studies in Ancient Oriental Civilization, no. 32. Chicago: Univ. of
    Chicago Press, 1963.
Goitein, S. D.
    'Našim K^e yoṣrot Suge Sifrut Bammiqra'.' *In 'iyyunim Bammiqra'.* Tel
    Aviv: Yavneh, 1967, pp. 248-317.
Good, Edwin M.
    'Ezekiel's Ship: Some Extended Metaphors in the Old Testament.'
    Semitics, 1 (1970), 79-103.
Gordis, Robert.
    The Song of Songs: A Study, Modern Translation and Commentary. New
    York: The Jewish Theological Seminary of America, 1961.
Gray, George Buchanan.
    *The Forms of Hebrew Poetry: Considered with Special Reference to the
    Criticism and Interpretation of the Old Testament.* 1st ed., 1915; rpt.
    with Prolegomenon by David Noel Freedman. New York: Ktav
    Publishing House, 1972.
The Holy Bible
    (Authorized or King James Version). London, 1611.
The Holy Bible: Revised Standard Version.
    New York: Thomas Nelson & Sons, 1946-52.
The Holy Scriptures According to the Masoretic Text: A New Translation.
    With the Aid of Previous Versions and with Constant Consultation of
    Jewish Authorities. Philadelphia: The Jewish Publication Society of
    America, 1917.
Jacobsen, Thorkild, and Wilson, John A., trans.
    Most Ancient Verse. Introduction by David Grene. Chicago: The
    Oriental Institute of the University of Chicago, 1963.
The Jerusalem Bible.
    Ed. Alexander Jones. Garden City: Doubleday & Company, 1966.
Kittel, Rudolph, ed.
    Biblia Hebraica. Textum masoreticum curavit Paul Kahle. Editionem
    tertiam denuo elaboratam ad finum perduxerunt A. Alt and O.
    Eissfeldt, 1937. 7th ed. Stuttgart: Wurttembergische Bibelanstalt, 1951.
Koehler, Ludwig, and Baumgartner, Walter.
    Lexicon in Veteris Testamenti Libros. 2nd ed. Leiden: E. J. Brill, 1958.
Kosmala, Hans.
    'Form and Structure in Ancient Hebrew Poetry (A New Approach).'
    Vetus Testamentum, 14 (1964), 423-445; *Vetus Testamentum,* 16 (1966),
    152-180.
Kramer, Samuel Noah.
    *The Sacred Marriage Rite: Aspects of Faith, Myth, and Ritual in Ancient
    Sumer.* Bloomington and London: Indiana Univ. Press, 1969.
Krinetzki, Leo, O.S.B.
    *Das Hohe Lied: Kommentar zu Gestalt und Kerygma eines alttestament-
    liche Liebesliedes.* Kommentar und Beiträge zum Alten und Neuen
    Testament. Dusseldorf: Patmos-Verlag, 1964.

Landsberger, Franz.
    'Poetic Units Within the Song of Songs.' *Journal of Biblical Literature*, 73 (1954), 203-216.
Landy, Francis.
    'Beauty and the Enigma: An Inquiry into Some Interrelated Episodes of the Song of Songs.' *Journal for the Study of the Old Testament*, 17 (1980), 55-106.
——— 'The Song of Songs and the Garden of Eden.' *Journal of Biblical Literature*, 98 (1979), 513-528.
Lord, Albert.
    The Singer of Tales. Cambridge, Mass.: Harvard Univ. Press, 1960.
Lys, Daniel.
    Le Plus Beau Chant de la Création: Commentaire du Cantique des Cantiques. Lectio Divina, 51. Paris: Les Éditions du Cerf, 1968.
Mandelkern, Solomon.
    Veteris Testamenti Concordantiae Hebraice Atque Chaldaicae. 2 vols. 2nd ed., 1937; rpt. Graz: Akademische Druck- U. Verlagsanstalt, 1955.
May, H. G.
    'Some Cosmic Connotations of *Mayim Rabbim*, "Many Waters." ' *Journal of Biblical Literature*, 74 (1955), 9-21.
McMichael, James.
    The Style of the Short Poem. Belmont, Ca.: Wadsworth Publishing Co., 1967.
Meek, Theophile J.
    'The Song of Songs: Introduction and Exegesis.' In *The Interpreter's Bible*. Ed. George A. Buttrick. New York: Abington Press, 1956, vol. V, pp. 91-148.
Moffatt, James, trans.
    A New Translation of the Bible. Rev. ed. New York and London: Harper & Brothers, 1935.
Moldenke, Harold N., and Moldenke, Alma L.
    Plants of the Bible. New York: Ronald Press Co., 1952.
Muilenburg, James.
    'Form Criticism and Beyond.' *Journal of Biblical Literature*, 88 (1969), 1-18.
——— 'A Study in Hebrew Rhetoric: Repetition and Style.' In *Congress Volume, Copenhagen, 1953*. Supplements to Vetus Testamentum, vol. I. Leiden: E. J. Brill, 1953, pp. 97-111.
Murphy, Roland.
    'Towards a Commentary on the Song of Songs.' *Catholic Biblical Quarterly*, 39 (1977), 482-496.
The New American Bible.
    Translated from the Original Languages with Critical Use of All the Ancient Sources by Members of the Catholic Biblical Association of America. New York: P. J. Kennedy & Sons, 1970.
The New English Bible: The Old Testament.
    Oxford: Oxford Univ. Press and Cambridge: Cambridge Univ. Press, 1970.

Nielsen, Eduard.
  Oral Tradition: A Modern Problem in Old Testament. Foreword by H.
  H. Rowley. Studies in Biblical Theology, 11. Chicago: Alec R. Allenson,
  Inc.; London, SCM Press, 1954.
P. E. N. American Center.
  *The World of Translation: Papers Delivered at the Conference on
  Literary Translation Held in New York City in May 1970.* New York:
  n.p., 1971.
Pfeiffer, Robert H.
  Introduction to the Old Testament. 2nd ed. New York: Harper &
  Brothers, 1948.
Pope, Marvin H.
  'A Mare in Pharaoh's Chariotry.' *Bulletin of the American Schools of
  Oriental Research,* No. 200 (December, 1970), pp. 56-61.
—— *The Song of Songs: A New Translation with Introduction and Commentary.*
  New York: Doubleday, 1977.
Pound, Ezra, and Stock, Noel, trans.
  Love Poems of Ancient Egypt. New York: New Directions, 1962.
Pritchard, James B., ed.
  Ancient Near Eastern Texts Relating to the Old Testament. 3rd ed. with
  supplement. Princeton: Princeton Univ. Press, 1969.
Rabin, Chaim.
  'The Song of Songs and Tamil Poetry.' *Studies in Religion,* 3 (1973-4),
  205-219.
Rauber, D. F.
  'Literary Values in the Bible: The Book of Ruth.' *Journal of Biblical
  Literature,* 89 (1970), 27-37.
Richards, Ivor Armstrong.
  Practical Criticism: A Study of Literary Judgment. 1st ed. 1929; rpt.
  New York: Harcourt, Brace and Co., 1954.
Ringgren, Helmer.
  Das Hohe Lied. Das Altes Testament Deutsch, vol. XVI, pp. 257-293.
  2nd ed. Göttingen: Vandenhoeck & Ruprecht, 1967.
Robert, A., P.S.S. and Tournay, R., O.P.
  Le Cantique des Cantique: Traduction et Commentaire. Avec le
  Concours de A. Feuillet, P.S.S. Études Bibliques. Paris: J. Gabalda et
  Cie., 1963.
Robinson, Theodore H.
  'Hebrew Poetic Form: The English Tradition.' In *Congress Volume,
  Copenhagen, 1953.* Supplements to Vetus Testamentum, vol. I.
  London: E. J. Brill, 1953, pp. 128-149.
—— *The Poetry of the Old Testament.* London: Gerald Duckworth & Co.,
  1947.
Rosenzweig, Franz.
  The Star of Redemption. Trans. from the 2nd ed. of 1930 by William W.
  Hallo. Foreward by N. N. Glatzer. Boston: Beacon Press, 1972.
Rowley, H. H.
  'The Interpretation of the Song of Songs.' In *The Servant of the Lord*

and other Essays on the Old Testament. 2nd ed. Oxford: Basil Blackwell, 1965, pp. 197-245.

—— 'The Meaning of "The Shulammite." ' *American Journal of Semitic Languages and Literatures,* 56 (1930), 84-91.

Rudolph, Wilhelm.
Das Buch Ruth; Das Hohe Lied; Die Klagelieder. Kommentar zum Alten Testament, vol. XVII, 1-3. Gütersloh: Gütersloher Verlagshaus Gerd Mohn, 1962.

Schoff, Wilfred H., ed.
The Song of Songs: A Symposium. Philadelphia: The Commercial Museum, 1924.

Scholem, Gershom.
'At the Completion of Buber's Translation of the Bible.' Trans. Michael A. Meyer. In *The Messianic Idea in Judaism and Other Essays on Jewish Spirituality.* New York: Schocken Books, 1971, pp. 314-319.

—— ed. *Zohar: The Book of Splendor.* New York: Schocken Books, 1963.

Segal, M. H.
'The Song of Songs.' *Vetus Testamentum,* 12 (1962), 470-490.

Segert, Stanislav.
'Problems of Hebrew Prosody.' In *Congress Volume, Oxford, 1959.* Supplements to Vetus Testamentum, vol. VII. Leiden: E. J. Brill, 1960, pp. 283-291.

Simpson, William Kelly, ed.
The Literature of Ancient Egypt: An Anthology of Stories, Instructions, and Poetry. New ed. With translations by R. O. Faulkner, Edward F. Wente, Jr., and William Kelly Simpson. New Haven and London: Yale Univ. Press, 1973.

Smith, Barbara Herrnstein.
Poetic Closure: A Study of How Poems End. Chicago. Univ. of Chicago Press, 1968.

Smith, J. M. Powis et al., trans.
The Complete Bible: An American Translations: The Old Testament. Chicago: Univ. of Chicago Press, 1939.

Soulen, Richard N.
'The *Wasfs* of the Song of Songs and Hermeneutic.' *Journal of Biblical Literature,* 86 (1967), 183-190.

Spitzer, Leo.
'Linguistics and Literary History.' In *Linguistics and Literary History: Essays in Stylistics.* Princeton: Princeton Univ. Press, 1948, pp. 1-39.

Steiner, George, ed.
Introduction to *The Penguin Book of Modern Verse Translation.* Baltimore: Penguin Books, 1966, pp. 21-36.

Trible, Phyllis.
'Depatriarchalizing in Biblical Interpretation.' *Journal of the American Academy of Religion,* 41 (1973), 30-48.

God and the Rhetoric of Sexuality. Philadelphia: Fortress Press, 1978.

Wakeman, Mary, ed.
'Images of Women in the Bible.' (Contributors: Mary Callaway, Cheryl

Exum, Marianne Micks, Mary Wakeman, and Martha Wilson.)
Women's Caucus-Religious Studies Newsletter, Vol. 2, No. 3 (fall, 1974),
pp. 1, 3-6, 10.

Waterman, Leroy.
The Song of Songs: Translated and Interpreted as a Dramatic Poem. Ann
Arbor: Univ. of Michigan Press, 1948.

Webster, Edwin C.
'Pattern in the Song of Songs.' *Journal for the Study of the Old
Testament*, 22 (1982), pp. 73-93.

Wetzstein, J. G. von.
'Die syrische Dreschtafel.' *Zeitschrift für Ethnologie*, 5 (1873), 270-302.

Whallon, William.
'Formulaic Poetry in the Old Testament.' *Comparative Literature*, 15
(1963), 1-14.

Yip, Wai-lim.
'The Chinese Poem: Some Aspects of the Problem of Syntax in
Translation.' In *Ezra Pound's Cathay*. Princeton: Princeton Univ.
Press, 1969, pp. 8-33.

Yoder, Perry.
'A-B Pairs and Oral Composition in Hebrew Poetry.' *Vetus Testamentum*,
21 (1971), 470-489.

—— 'Biblical Hebrew.' In *Versification: Major Language Types*. Ed. W. K.
Wimsatt. New York: New York Univ. Press, 1972, pp. 52-65.

Zohary, Michael, and Feinbrun, Naomi.
Flora Palaestina. 2 vols. Jerusalem: Israel Academy of Sciences and
Humanities, 1966.